THE
Ships

A Guide to Finding Your Immigrant Ancestor's Arrival Record

Also by Robert Paoletta

Finding Italian Roots:
The Complete Guide for Americans

Only a Few Bones:
A True Account of the Rolling Fork Tragedy
and Its Aftermath

THEY CAME IN
Ships

A Guide to Finding
Your Immigrant
Ancestor's Arrival
Record

Third Edition
Updated and Revised

John Philip Colletta, Ph.D.

Ancestry.

Library of Congress Cataloging-in-Publication Data

Colletta, John Philip.
  They came in ships : a guide to finding your immigrant ancestor's
arrival record / by John Philip Colletta.—Rev., updated, 3rd ed.
    p. cm.
  Includes bibliographical references and index.
  ISBN 0-916489-37-X (alk. paper)
  1. Ships—United States—Passenger lists—Handbooks, manuals, etc. 2.
United States—Genealogy—Handbooks, manuals, etc. I. Title.
  CS49 .C63 2002
  929'.1'072073—dc21

                                                        2002006461

Published by Ancestry® Publishing, an
imprint of MyFamily.com, Inc.

P.O. Box 990
Orem, Utah 84059
www.ancestry.com

First Printing 2002
10 9 8 7 6 5 4 3 2 1

Printed in the United States of America

Contents

Conclusion

Preface

They came in ships. How else could they get here—the Europeans, Africans, Asians who arrived from the late sixteenth century through the mid-twentieth century? They came in sailing vessels and steamships to Atlantic, Pacific, Great Lakes, and Gulf Coast ports. Every ship had her passenger list or cargo manifest, and many of these records—which identify the immigrants on board and when they came—have survived. When no such list has survived—for sixteenth-, seventeenth-, and eighteenth-century arrivals, most particularly—a variety of other types of public records often provide information about when immigrants came and on what ship. Even for those people who immigrated overland from Canada, 1895 through 1954, and Mexico, about 1905 through about 1955, arrival records are readily accessible.[1]

Most Americans can discover what ship brought their ancestors to this continent, or at least the date or year when they arrived, and where. Your search may be easy and result in quick success, or it may be a challenge requiring time and persistence. Every ancestor's story is unique, so every search for an ancestor's ship is unique. By following the instructions explained in this book, however, chances are excellent that you will eventually discover the immigration facts for at least some, if not all, of your forebears from overseas.

Books, articles, CD-ROMs, and Internet websites about ship passenger lists abound, and more appear every year. Some are bibliographies of lists that have been transcribed in books or on websites. Some are alphabetical indexes to the names appearing in selected lists, published and unpublished. Some describe the experience of immigrating to America, or discuss the old sailing vessels and steamships that

---

[1] Regarding documentation, see Bibliographic Note on page 133.

brought the immigrants. Some deal with particular ethnic or national or religious groups, and the specific periods and ports of their immigration stories. However, prior to the publication of this book, there was no manual to explain to the family researcher exactly how to use the wealth of materials available to locate a particular individual named in an old ship passenger list. This book was written specifically to fill that need: to help you find one immigrant among the millions.

Published originally in 1989, this manual was first updated and expanded in 1993. Since then, continued interest on the part of the American public has fueled sustained publication of materials dealing with arrival records. In addition to many more books and magazine articles, numerous pertinent websites have appeared on the Internet, and materials in CD-ROM format have entered the market, too. This country's ever-growing number of family historians—as well as casual visitors to Ellis Island—has expressed a desire for more instruction on how to search for an immigrant ancestor's ship, especially among the arrival records that are not indexed. Therefore, in response to the plethora of new materials and the persistent demand on the part of the public, this third edition has been prepared. The bibliography has been expanded to reflect the current state of both traditional and electronic resources, and the instructional text has been updated to make the fullest use of these resources to find the ship passenger list—or other record—that bears your immigrant ancestor's name and arrival information. The author thanks his friend and colleague, Kory Meyerink, A.G., for his meticulous reading of the manuscript of this third edition, as well as for his expert observations and excellent suggestions, which helped make the finished product a better one.

First of all, the introduction shows how you can extract much more from a passenger list than just the name of your ancestor's ship and date of arrival. The diverse data contained in passenger lists can be understood, interpreted, and combined with other information about your ancestors to advance and expand your genealogical knowledge and enhance your family history. This third edition discusses new ways for you to do this. You want to get all you can out of your search!

Chapter 1 prepares you to undertake the search. It tells you not only what fundamental facts you need to know about your immigrant ancestor before beginning, but suggests where you may find that information as well. The text of this third edition addresses the common problem of surname changes and discusses additional sources—including Internet websites—for obtaining the information you need to get your search under way. To focus your efforts, the essential distinction is drawn between searching for arrival information recorded prior to 1820, and that recorded since 1820.

Chapters 2 and 3 guide you step-by-step through the research process, whether your immigrant ancestor arrived in a sailing vessel in the sixteenth, seventeenth, eighteenth or nineteenth century, or on board a steamship in the nineteenth or twentieth century. Specific strategies are suggested for sample research scenarios, and detailed instruction is given on how to use the indexes and resource materials at your disposal to overcome obstacles to your search. This third edition contains expanded discussions of colonial period immigrant records and port-by-port peculiarities of the federal records.

Chapter 4 addresses how to search for a ship when your ancestor arrived during a year that is not included in any National Archives index. It explores alternative resources—the entire section on CD-ROM indexes and Internet websites is new to this edition—and demonstrates through a variety of sample research scenarios how to use each of these resources. No methodology goes unexplored! Nor do you have to go to Washington, D.C., to use the many National Archives microfilm publications mentioned in this book. Many of them are also available at the thirteen Regional Archives throughout the United States, and all of them are in the collection of the Latter-day Saints Family History Library (LDS Family History Library) in Salt Lake City, Utah. With the LDS Family History Library's microfilm loan program, all of the micropublications may be borrowed and examined at any one of thousands of Family Research Centers worldwide. Major libraries across the country also own much of the microfilm, as well as many of the books, discussed in this manual. In addition, more and more of the resources discussed here are appearing online at Internet websites, too. Indeed, passenger arrival records have never been so readily and so broadly searchable as they are today!

Chapter 5 examines a selection of materials and information helpful for finding the arrival records of ancestors who immigrated under various particular circumstances. For example, the section on immigrants who arrived in the United States via Canada has been expanded, and a new section has been added that addresses records of people coming across the border from Mexico. Laws regulating immigration during the 1920s are explained because they might suggest a research strategy you would never have thought to consider. Where and how to obtain pictures of your ancestors' ships is also discussed.

Throughout the text of this manual the author shares many specific and helpful hints, warnings and suggestions based on his twenty years of experience researching ship passenger lists and lecturing on them at the National Archives. How to decipher illegible microfilm, determine your ancestor's most likely port of departure and port of arrival, use the newspapers of the port city, discover births and deaths at sea, know how long it took a sailing ship, or a steamship, to cross the Atlantic, learn whether your ancestor was a stowaway, a member of the ship's crew, obtain a picture of your ancestor's vessel—these are just a few of the numerous issues addressed based on the author's personal experience. Any of this information, sooner or later in your search, may become indispensable to locating your ancestor's ship.

The conclusion of this third edition provides an expanded discussion of Ellis Island, because persistent myths and misunderstandings about that immigrant processing station continue to impede the genealogical inquiry of many Americans. Though millions of Americans are descended from immigrants who arrived at New York, not all of those immigrants passed through Ellis Island. The conclusion shows how Ellis Island fits into the larger history of the port of New York, and helps you appreciate your forebear's actual—not imagined!—Immigration story.

Following the text is a select bibliography—updated and expanded for this third edition to include 130 works—because undertaking the search for your ancestor's ship requires a familiarity with the available resources. The annotations in the bibliography help you determine at a glance whether any particular work may be useful in your search.

This manual closes with the chart "How to Find Your Immigrant Ancestor's Ship," which was originally prepared by the author for the National Park Service as a part of the Ellis Island exhibit "The Peopling of America: Four Hundred Years of Immigration History." (Although the information provided in the chart was used in a different format.) The chart summarizes graphically the key research strategies presented in this manual, allowing you to focus immediately on the method most appropriate to your own personal search.

For it is your search—your journey to the genesis of your family in the New World. It is a quest that yields personal satisfaction, knowledge, and joy. Here's how you do it…

Introduction

What Passenger Lists Tell You About Your Ancestors

With the founding of Saint Augustine, Florida, in 1565, by the Spanish, Europeans began to settle permanently in the New World. Henceforth ships would bring not only explorers and soldiers and traders and priests and seasonal fishermen—as they had already been doing for some decades—but entire families of men, women, and children who intended to spend the rest of their lives in North America. For this reason, 1565 is a logical beginning date for a manual on finding an ancestor's ship.

The closing of Ellis Island in 1954 provides a logical ending date. It was during the 1950s that increasing numbers of immigrants began traveling to North America not in ships, but in airplanes. By the late 1960s, most immigrants were arriving by air.

Generally, for each voyage that a ship made to America between 1565 and 1954, a passenger list was compiled. The list is usually headed with the name of the ship, the captain's name, the port and date of her departure, and the port and date of her arrival in America. Beneath this heading is a roster of the passengers on board. In addition, almost all lists include some personal information about each passenger besides his or her name. Exactly what other information was included has varied widely over the past four hundred years, as this manual will demonstrate in detail in chapters 2 and 3.

1

Lists composed prior to 1893, especially those of the colonial period, may appear at first glance to be disappointingly sparse in informational content. After that date, in compliance with U.S. law, they contain an increasing amount of personal and family data about each passenger. As you evaluate the few facts given in an early list, or the more plentiful data supplied in a later list, within the larger context of history—especially in light of your previous genealogical findings—they can add up to much more family information than the bare statistics themselves. For this reason, before examining the content of ship passenger lists in detail, it may be useful to consider the preliminary question: What can I expect to learn about my family from ship passenger lists? The answer is: More than you think … as long as you know what to look for!

To alert you to the kinds of questions you should have in mind as you conduct your search (and to whet your appetite for the wonderful world of ship passenger lists!), a sampling is given of just three ways in which the information that passenger lists reveal may determine the direction of your genealogical research and add colorful breadth to your ancestor's immigration story.

Biographical and Genealogical Information

Ship passenger lists may add rich biographical and genealogical details to your family history. For example, you may discover that your ancestor sailed to the American colonies with a royal governor or other prominent personage of the period, perhaps Benjamin Franklin or Thomas Jefferson, both of whom made many transatlantic crossings. Perhaps your ancestor crossed the Pacific from China at the age of fourteen—unaccompanied. Or perhaps your ancestor was a stowaway, or born at sea, or one of a group of young ladies sent to Louisiana as prospective wives for the unmarried settlers.

I discovered from ship lists of 1898 and 1902, for example, that a great-great-grandmother's third husband and then fourth husband—

both of whom I knew lived their entire lives in Sicily—had crossed the Atlantic and spent time in New York City with their children from previous marriages. This information dramatized for me the surprising mobility that even a poor family from a tiny Sicilian village could enjoy at the turn of the century. It showed how families separated by an ocean were able to keep in touch, thanks to the wondrous advances made by steam-powered transportation.

If your ancestors emigrated from Southern or Eastern Europe after 1921, you may discover that they booked passage to America on French steamships leaving from Le Havre rather than on vessels leaving from ports closer to home. Ship lists reveal that many southern and eastern Europeans devised schemes to circumvent the immigration restrictions imposed on them by the Emergency Quota Act of 1921 (See chapter 4). They were desperate to be reunited with husbands, wives, or children already established in the United States, and migrating to northern European port and sailing on a northern European liner seems to have resolved their dilemma.

All kinds of details about your ancestor's life, and the world in which he or she lived, may come to light from the passenger list.

The Overseas Link

Ship passenger lists may supply the vital transatlantic link you need to pursue your research overseas. You may find, for instance, that an ancestor with an English surname sailed from Glasgow, Scotland. This unexpected revelation would lead you to explore whether and when your ancestor's family had moved from England to Scotland, and enable you to pursue your research in a country you might never have imagined. Or a French Huguenot ancestor may show up in the passenger list of a Dutch ship out of Amsterdam, providing the clue you need to continue your research on that family in the Netherlands, before continuing your search in France.

My grandmother told me her mother had been born in the Sicilian town of Bagheria, but I was unable to discover a birth record for her there. Then I found her name in the passenger list of the ship that brought her to America and discovered that she had not been born in Bagheria, as my grandmother had always believed, but in the village of Castronovo. Writing a letter to the Catholic parish in Castronovo secured my great-grandmother's baptismal record and allowed me to continue to research her ancestry in that village.

The Migration Story

The facts of your immigrant ancestor's life and voyage take on fuller meaning when viewed within the context of his or her family. You may be able to deduce from the names included on the ship passenger list whether your ancestor was traveling alone or in the company of family members. Which brothers or sisters also came? Which ones stayed in the Old Country? Did your ancestor's entire extended family eventually immigrate—including cousins, uncles, and aunts? Did some relatives go back? Who? And why?

Your ancestor might have been the adventurous trailblazer, the one who led the way for the rest of his family to follow. Or your ancestor may have been the last to come, the one reluctant to give up the land and culture of birth until necessity imposed the decision. Ship lists reveal how your ancestor fit into the migration story of his or her family, and how the migration story of your family fit into the larger saga of the building of America.

The list of the ship *Nile*, which sailed into New York Harbor from Le Havre, France, in 1830, taught me that a fifty-one-year-old ancestor of mine had traveled to the United States not only with all of his own children, their spouses, and *their* children, but with all of his families-in-law as well! They were all residents of the same village in the province of Lorraine, and they had evidently chosen to lighten the burdens and risks of crossing the Atlantic in a small sailing vessel by sharing those burdens and risks—under the leadership of the clan's elderly *paterfamilias*, my ancestor.

With the age of steam, young men from Europe were able to travel to the United States and home again annually to satisfy this country's seasonal demand for labor. They came in the spring and left before winter, earning the sobriquet "birds of passage." By their second or third voyage, many of these workers were bringing their wives and children with them to settle in the United States. Some families went back and forth across the Atlantic a number of times before remaining here for good. Passenger lists help establish not only the composition of these families—which children were born where and when—but also a chronology of their travels and a fuller understanding of what immigrating meant to them.

Biographical and genealogical information, the transatlantic link, and your family's migration story represent just a sampling of the numerous ways in which information from ship passenger lists may be used to expand your research activities and your knowledge of your family's history. So, how do you get to that passenger list?

Chapter One

What You Need to Know and Where to Find It

All genealogical research is a dogged progression from the known to the unknown. You begin with a few known facts and use them to discover more facts in the old records. Then you use that newly found information to progress back another step in time, and another, and another. Therefore, before beginning the search for your immigrant ancestor's ship, you should be aware of what facts you need to know and where to find them.

Basic Facts You Must Know about the Passenger

Full Original Name

You must know your immigrant ancestor's full original name—given name as well as surname. Discovering this may present a challenge since many American families do not go by the same family name as their immigrant ancestor. You may spell your name in a slightly different way. It might be an anglicized or shortened version, or a transliteration of the original. Perhaps your surname is even a literal English translation of your ancestor's name. The historical vagaries that caused surnames to change are numerous, and you are far from alone if your family name is not the same as your immigrant ancestor's. Nevertheless, whatever your personal story may be, you must learn what your immigrant ancestor's full name was in the Old Country before you can begin your search.

This information is required because passenger lists were prepared in the port of embarkation before the ship sailed. During colonial times, ship captains and ship companies devised whatever lists they deemed necessary for their purposes. Beginning in 1820, when U.S. law dictated what information had to be included on every list, blank lists were printed and sold to ship companies by private printers in the United States. From 1891 on into the twentieth century the U.S. government printed the blank lists and distributed them to the ship companies, which took them to their respective ports overseas to be completed for each voyage, normally by the ship's purser. As a result, the printed words—the opening sentences at the top of the first page and all of the column headings—are in English. But the handwritten names appear as the ship's purser penned them on the list.

Though some pursers may have transcribed each passenger's name from passports or travel papers or other identification, it appears that often—before the twentieth century, at least—pursers simply asked the passengers their names and wrote them down as they heard them. The errors that resulted from this practice were inevitable, especially with surnames transliterated from non-Latin alphabets, such as Russian, Ukrainian, Chinese, Hebrew, and Japanese. Take, for example, a Jewish tailor from Kiev who is leaving from Bremen on a ship of the North German Lloyd Line around 1905 (as thousands did). Though he is unschooled, he can recognize and perhaps even sign his own name, but only in the Cyrillic alphabet, or perhaps in Hebrew. He has no familiarity whatsoever with the Latin alphabet. When he tells his name to the German purser filling out the passenger list, the official immediately romanizes the name, putting it into Latin letters as he hears and understands it. Naturally, the Jewish emigrant is unable to correct the purser's transliteration if it is not correct. This explains why three brothers coming from the Ukraine on three different ships might end up using three different variants of their family name.

Even surnames and given names from languages that use the Latin alphabet are sometimes corrupted on passenger lists. For instance, many ships of American and British lines embarked from the port of Le Havre on the northern coast of France. The purser was normally an American or Englishman whose work and travels had provided him with a rudimentary knowledge of French and German. When hearing and writing down the names of French and German passengers, therefore, the purser might translate into English a name whose meaning he knew—turning Pierre into Peter, for example, or Schmidt into Smith. Or he might translate the French La Fontaine to Fountain, or the German Vogel to Bird; or drop the umlaut from Müller and write down Mueller or Miller, or just Muller. The officer might simply do the best he could to spell unfamiliar names as they sounded to him—and French, if not German, is a distinctly unphonetic language. Unschooled French and German emigrants were in no position to correct the purser's transcription of their names.

When searching for an immigrant ancestor's ship, therefore, always bear in mind a few possible variant spellings of the surname. You may need all of them to find your ancestor! If your ancestor habitually used a nickname, make note of that, too, because he may be listed under the nickname if that is the name he told the purser.

It is important to remember that women in some continental European countries, such as France, Italy, and the Netherlands (though not Germany), conduct matters of record under their maiden names. Therefore, they are often listed in nineteenth- and twentieth-century passenger lists under their maiden names, even though they may have been married, and in the company of their husband or children. This generally holds true when they are traveling on a French or Italian liner; however, lists of steamships of other registries may not reflect this custom. Moreover, in French passenger lists of the colonial period, you will find married women using their husband's surname.

If you suspect your ancestor was traveling in the company of a relative or neighbor, note the surname of that relative or neighbor. The traveling partner's name could be crucial to finding your own ancestor, as chapter 3 will explain.

Approximate Age at Arrival

You must know the approximate age of your immigrant ancestor when he or she arrived. This information is required to distinguish him or her from other immigrants with the same name. Not hundreds, not thousands, but millions of immigrants came to America between 1565 and 1954! So, when searching ship passenger lists, you may discover that a name you thought was unique, or at least rare, was actually very common. Many ethnic and national groups around the world observed rigid traditions for naming their children; generation after generation, the same names reappear. Knowing your immigrant ancestor's approximate age upon arrival is essential.

Approximate Date of Arrival

You must know the approximate date of your ancestor's arrival in America in order to know where to start. If you can learn the year, and perhaps the season of the year, or even the specific month, you are well prepared to begin your search. But knowing only an approximate year—a span of maybe three or four years—is sufficient to get you started. However, the closer you can get to an actual date (month, day, year), the better your chances of success.

Additional Facts about the Immigration

While the preceding "starting information" is often enough to lead you to an ancestor's arrival record, knowing an additional fact or two about the immigrant and his or her migration story is always helpful, and sometimes critical, particularly when searching "unindexed years." The immigrant's ethnic heritage or nationality, for example, or the port from which he or she departed, or the port of arrival—such information facilitates the search. A small, seemingly insignificant detail may turn out to be the decisive lead you need to identify the right ship. It may distinguish your ancestor from another passenger of the exact same name and age. It may narrow the approximate arrival period down to a searchable number of years. Passenger lists created prior to the end of the nineteenth century contain so little personal information about each individual on board that an additional fact or two may be essential to corroborate that you have indeed found your ancestor. Some familiarity with the native place the immigrant ancestor left, when he or she left it—particularly the prevailing emigration patterns—is also helpful. As with all genealogical investigation, the more knowledge you bring to the search, the better your chances of success.

Where Can You Find This Information?

There is no point in searching for your immigrant ancestor's ship until you have a good idea of the following: (1) your ancestor's full original name, (2) approximate age at arrival, (3) approximate date of arrival, and (4) perhaps an additional fact or two about his or her migration experience. So where can you discover this information?

Oral Family Tradition

Has a story about your immigrant ancestor been passed down from generation to generation within your family—perhaps containing the name of the ship? Was your ancestor a member of the crew who "jumped ship" when the vessel pulled into the U.S. port? Did your ancestor from the sunny Mediterranean basin arrive in snow-covered Boston with no winter clothing? Did your Scandinavian ancestor arrive at Baltimore on a sweltering August afternoon with only heavy woolen clothing to wear? Perhaps your ancestor arrived in America on Christmas Day, or the 4th of July. Or was your ancestor's ship detained in quarantine because a case of cholera had been discovered on board? Possibly your ancestor entered New York in the late nineteenth century but did not pass through Ellis Island.

No matter how farfetched family lore may sound, it almost always holds a kernel of truth. And that kernel of truth, however small, could provide the essential clue that leads you to your ancestor's ship. No matter how insignificant the details of the oral tradition may seem, one of those details could be the hint that rewards your search with success. So take note of every family story you hear!

Nevertheless, bear in mind that family stories do become skewed over generations of retelling. They tend to inflate the importance of the ancestor, or romanticize the ancestor's experience through elaborated details and commonplace fictions. Be skeptical. The kernel of truth in immigration stories is sometimes hard to find.

Personal and Family Documents

Personal and family documents may yield one or all of the three essential facts you need. These include passports and travel papers, family letters, diaries, Bible inscriptions, death announcements of relations who stayed in the Old Country, funeral remembrance cards, obituaries clipped from newspapers, wedding invitations, birth and christening announcements, steamship ticket stubs, and U.S. Health Service Inspection Cards, certificates of naturalization and citizenship class diplomas, and other similar mementoes linked to the immigration generation.

If your family has been in the United States only two or three generations, you might find such keepsakes in the attic or basement of your parents' home, or in the possession of a relative. Old family photographs that have been labeled by a thoughtful great-aunt or uncle may provide the information you seek. Even if your family immigrated in the early seventeenth century, you may still discover some treasured document about the immigrant ancestor. When interviewing relatives about your family's origins in America, be sure to ask: Who has any old family photos? Are there any heirlooms from the Old Country still in the family? Who might have inherited some old family documents? Contact that lucky kinsperson immediately!

Civil and Religious Records

Civil records of birth, marriage and death, probate records, and military service records may be found in archives, courthouses, and libraries around the United States. In addition, churches keep records of baptisms, marriages, and burials, and synagogues have maintained records of congregation membership and burials. There are tombstone inscriptions, too, at the cemetery. Any one of these resources, or a combination of them, may give you the essential facts you seek.

Federal censuses may also be helpful, especially if your immigrant ancestor was living in the United States in 1900, 1910, 1920 or 1930. In those years the census takers asked foreign-born residents what year they came to the United States, how many years they had resided here, and what their citizenship status was. Federal censuses are available at the National Archives in Washington, D.C., the thirteen Regional Archives, and numerous libraries nationwide, including the LDS Family History Library. They are also increasingly available online. The 1900 and 1920 censuses are fully indexed by head of household and unrelated individuals; the 1910 census, however, is indexed for only twenty-one states. If an ancestor of yours immigrated during the 1920s, the 1930 federal census is a good place to start, and there are name indexes to eleven southern states.

State censuses may provide the same information for an earlier period. Facts about a foreign-born resident's year of immigration and citizenship status appear on many nineteenth-century state censuses long before they appear on federal censuses. To cite but one example, the 1855 New York State census contains such data. State censuses are available in your state archives, library, or historical society, and in many local libraries, too.

If your immigrant ancestor became a U.S. citizen, the record of his or her naturalization may contain the facts you need to find the arrival record. Naturalization records sometimes include not only the year of immigration and the individual's age at that time, but the name of the ship and the port and date of arrival as well. The amount and type of information given in naturalization records varies widely, however. Naturalization records made in federal courts are available either at the National Archives or one of its thirteen Regional Archives. Naturalizations made in state courts are found in state level archives and county courthouses. Naturalizations made in municipal courts are generally preserved in the city archives.

If your immigrant ancestor, after being naturalized, applied to the U.S. State Department for a passport, the passport application will contain the facts about his immigration and naturalization. Since passports were not required by law until 1941 (except for two brief periods), most Americans did not bother to apply for one. Many others did, however, including naturalized citizens returning to their homelands to visit relatives. Passport applications from 1791 through 1925 are available on microfilm, and there are registers and indexes to them.

Finally, if your immigrant ancestor took advantage of the Homestead Act of 1862 to obtain free land from the U.S. government, his homestead file will contain information about his immigration and naturalization. Homestead files are kept in the National Archives.

Published Works in Libraries

There are thousands of published genealogies, as well as state, county, city or town, or regional histories, from which you might learn your immigrant ancestor's name, age at arrival, and date of arrival. These works cover geographic areas all over the United States, and time periods from the sixteenth through the twentieth centuries. New ones are being published continually (the American Bicentennial Celebration of 1976 provided renewed impetus), and old ones are appearing in reprint editions. In addition, multi-volume "American national biography" sets printed in the late nineteenth and early twentieth centuries—usually comprising one volume per state—contain sketches of the lives of many immigrant pioneers. Histories of counties, cities, towns, and regions—with their tighter geographical focus—include biographical information about many local residents who are not even mentioned in the larger state histories.

Also numerous and growing in number and diversity are histories that chronicle the appearance and growth of ethnic and national groups throughout the United States. Easily accessible are books about the Italians of St. Louis, the Polish community of Chicago, the Irish of Boston, the Jews of Miami, the Cajuns in Louisiana, the Germans in early Erie County, New York, and many, many others. For example, researchers of Bohemian ancestors have resources like:

Rosicky, Rose, comp. *A History of the Czechs (Bohemians) in Nebraska.* Omaha, Neb.: Czech Historical Society of Nebraska, 1929. Reprint by Unigraphic, Evanston, Ind., 1977.

Benes, Frank. *Czechs in Manitowoc County, Wisconsin, 1847-1932.* Manitowoc, Wis.: Manitowoc County Historical Society, 1979.

For immigrant ancestors who settled in urban areas, city directories—many of which have been published annually since the early 1800s—constitute a valuable tool. Noting when the immigrant first appears in the directory provides a rough "starting year" for the search for his or her arrival record. There are also ethnic professional directories, too, such as this one:

Directory of Italian-Americans in Commerce and Professions. Chicago: Continental Press, 1937.

Internet Websites and E-mail

The website of The Church of Jesus Christ of Latter-day Saints <www.familysearch.org> contains excellent and useful information about identifying immigrant ancestors. Among several enormous databases searchable at that site, the International Genealogical Index includes names and information about many thousands of immigrants. Other websites worth visiting, to name but two of the larger ones, include <www.cyndislist.com> and <www.ancestry.com>.

More and more family historians are now publishing the results of their research on the Internet, too, at huge international umbrella sites, or small, personal web pages. It may be that a relative of yours has already traced a branch of your family back to the immigrant, and this may supply the facts you need to begin your search for the ancestor's ship. Genealogists of the computer age are also taking full advantage of online "bulletin boards," "chat rooms," and e-mail for networking with distant kin around the country—indeed, around the world. Take full advantage of the new electronic tools, but beware! When accessing information on the Internet, be sure to look for the source cited for that piece of information, then consult that source to double-check for accuracy. While the Internet contains many gems for seekers of ancestors, it is rife with errors and misinformation. Always be skeptical!

Consult a manual on genealogy for more details concerning oral family tradition, family documents, civil and religious records, published works in libraries, and Internet websites and e-mail. Learn whether other resources might exist that will supply the three fundamental facts you need to begin your search for an ancestor's ship. Books and websites on genealogical sources and methods are numerous and provide information about where records are held, what information they contain, and how to gain access to them. The bibliography at the back of this book lists several such how-to and reference books and URLs. You can come up with the facts you need!

The Two Major Periods of Passenger Arrival Records

Records of people arriving on American shores may be divided into two periods: those earlier than 1820, and those of 1820 and later. How you conduct your search will be determined by whether your ancestor arrived before or since 1820.

Prior to 1820

If your ancestor arrived prior to 1820, any original passenger list bearing his or her name that may still exist might be found in any archive, museum, courthouse, basement or attic in this country or overseas (likely Spain, France, or Great Britain). Lists of this early period are not preserved in the National Archives. In fact, there is no central depository of any kind where pre-1820 passenger lists are gathered together and preserved, and the vast majority of them have long since disappeared. Chances of locating an original pre-1820 ship's passenger list are extremely slim. Fortunately for American family historians, however, many of the extant lists—perhaps most of them—have appeared over the years in published form. In addition, other kinds of early records—some colonial land grants, for example—may provide information about when immigrants came, and on what ship, and these, too, have been published in books, scholarly and genealogical journals, historical quarterlies, and other literature about the European settlement of America.

For the pre-1820 period, therefore, you will need to conduct your search in the library, using name indexes to published lists and other types of published arrival information. This process is explained in detail in chapter 2.

1820 and Later

If your ancestor arrived between 1820 and the mid-1950s, a microfilm copy of the passenger list bearing his or her name is probably (since not every list has survived the ravages of time) at the National Archives. The Family History Library in Salt Lake City has a copy of these enormous microfilm publications; the thirteen Regional Archives, as well as many major libraries across the country, have at least a portion of them. Furthermore, the passenger arrival lists for the port of New York, 1892 through 1924, have been digitized and are searchable online at <www.ellisislandrecords.com>.

For the period of 1820 and later, therefore, you will conduct your search in one or another of these repositories, using a variety of name indexes (microform, book, CD-ROM and online) to the microfilmed lists. This is explained in chapter 3. If the available indexes prove unhelpful, you will use the alternative resources and methods described in chapters 4 and 5.

Whether you are searching for a pre-1820 list that has been published, or an 1820-and-later list on microfilm or online, your method will involve two steps: (1) find your ancestor's name in one of the available name indexes to passenger arrival records; (2) using the information given in the index, locate and examine the list to confirm that the passenger with your ancestor's name is indeed your ancestor.

Note that the indexes you use are not physically attached to the passenger lists they index. They are separate, having been prepared many years after the creation of the lists by compilers and indexers to help researchers like yourself find a particular passenger. This means you may perform the first step of your search in one place, and then have to travel (or write) to another place to perform the second step.

Now that you have the fundamental facts you need, you can begin the search for your immigrant ancestor's passenger arrival record. You know your ancestor's full original name, approximate age at arrival, and approximate date of arrival, and you know whether your search will be in pre-1820 or 1820-and-later passenger lists. So on with the search!

Chapter Two

Passenger Arrival Information Prior to 1820

Published Pre-1820 Arrival (and Departure) Lists

Prior to 1820 there was no federal law requiring the recording of passenger arrival information in the United States. This explains why there are no passenger lists dated earlier than 1820 in the National Archives (with minor exceptions noted in chapter 3). Immigration matters were handled by the colonial powers—Spain, France, the Netherlands, England—and by the individual colonies, then later by the states, and sometimes even by the port cities themselves. Any records of incoming passengers considered necessary were maintained locally. Pre-1820 lists of passengers bound for or arriving in America have long since been lost, destroyed, or scattered into libraries, historical societies, museums, and archives throughout the United States and Europe. The Pennsylvania State Archives, for instance, holds captains' lists from 1727 through 1808 for the port of Philadelphia. This collection is a very happy and atypical instance, and it has been published (See Strassburger in the bibliography). As another example, archives in Madrid and Paris hold lists of ships leaving Spain and France (emigration or departure lists), heading for their colonies in North America.

Created by many different agencies, both domestic and foreign, over a span of years exceeding two centuries, these pre-1820 ship passenger lists vary broadly in the amount of information they contain.

Typically, they provide the ship's name; captain's name; date and port of embarkation, or date and port of arrival, or both; and the name of each passenger on board—though members of a family traveling with the head of household are not always named individually, but accounted for rather as, for instance, "with wife and two children," or "and household." The age of each passenger was also commonly given, as well as each one's country of origin, occupation, and sometimes the number of bags each passenger was carrying.

Many of these early arrival (and departure) lists have been published over the years—in state and local histories, historical society quarterlies, genealogical books and articles, scholarly studies about colonial America and immigration, and the like. Some are also appearing now on the Internet.

Published Works about Colonial Settlers

In addition to these published ship passenger lists, other kinds of colonial records may also contain information about when a settler first arrived in North America, including where and on what ship. These facts, though, since they are tangential to the specific purpose for which the record was created, tend to lie half-hidden, almost lost, in the larger document. For instance, colonial land grants, lists of indentured servants, oaths of allegiance, and pre-federal naturalization records may provide documentary evidence of new arrivals in America. Indeed, such records may constitute the only source of information about an immigrant ancestor who arrived prior to 1820, since many ship passenger lists of that early period no longer exist.

Many of these "alternative sources" of immigrant arrival information have appeared in print. For example, for the colony of Virginia:

Nugent, Nell Marion, comp. *Cavaliers and Pioneers: Abstracts of Virginia Land Patents and Grants, 1623–1732*. 3 vols.

Virginia Genealogical Society. *Cavaliers and Pioneers: Abstracts of Virginia Land Patents and Grants, 1733–1820.* 3 vols.

And for the colony of Maryland:

Skordas, Gust. *The Early Settlers of Maryland: An Index to Names of Immigrants Compiled from Records of Land Patents, 1633–1680, in the Hall of Records, Annapolis, Maryland.*

Gibb, Carson. *A Supplement to The Early Settlers of Maryland: 8,680 Entries Correcting Omissions and Errors in Gust Skordas's The Early Settlers of Maryland.*

And for the Delaware River Valley:

Johnson, Amandus. *The Swedish Settlements on the Delaware, 1638-1664.* 2 vols.

Also in print are emigration (departure) records of the colonial period, which document persons leaving their homelands for America. For example, for emigrants from England to Virginia:

Hotten, John Camden. *The Original Lists of Persons of Quality, 1600–1700.*

This classic work has been updated and expanded in an extensive series of books by Peter Wilson Coldham, beginning with:

The Complete Book of Emigrants, 1607–1776. 4 vols.

And for emigrants leaving Scotland:

Dobson, David. *Directory of Scottish Settlers in North America, 1625–1825.* 6 vols.

Bear in mind that works such as these are not comprehensive; they do not include every single immigrant or emigrant who falls within the scope of the title. Too often family researchers abandon the search when they do not find their immigrant's name listed in a book that appears to cover the right place and the right time period. These collections of colonial immigrants serve as a starting point for your search, but do not be deterred if your ancestor's name does not appear.

To find arrival information for an ancestor in the pre-1820 period, you must discover whether a passenger list with your ancestor's name on it, or some other record that happens to contain his or her arrival facts, has ever appeared in published form, and if it has, where and when, so that you may find it and examine it. You can do this by using the name indexes that have been created to these published materials.

Indexes to Published Arrival Information

Armed with your ancestor's full original name, approximate age at arrival, and approximate date of arrival, you are ready to charge into the library and attack the indexes to passenger arrival information. The bibliography at the end of this manual contains a wide selection of such indexes. Many of these works are more than just indexes, however, because they contain transcriptions or abstracts of the original lists. The transcribed or abstracted lists are usually printed in chronological order, and the name index to them is found in the back of the book. At this initial step in our search, we will focus on using the index portion of these works as an entree into the published arrival information.

Each index, each collection of transcriptions or abstracts, is different, because it was created according to the specific criteria set by the individual indexer or compiler. Each work covers only a particular port or ports, or a particular time period, or a particular ethnic, religious, or otherwise identifiable group. Therefore, before you use any of these, read the introductory material in the front of the volume carefully to understand precisely what is included in that volume: what exactly is indexed here, and how exactly is it indexed? Titles can be deceiving! To help you decide which books might be helpful to your personal search, the bibliography includes annotations that summarize what each work covers and how they differ from one another.

The first step to finding your immigrant ancestor's ship, therefore, is to search these indexes for your ancestor's name. If you are lucky enough to know an additional fact or two about your ancestor—such as nationality, or port of arrival, or that your ancestor was a member of an identifiable group, such as Mennonites or indentured servants, or where your immigrant ancestor first settled in the United States—you may bypass many of these indexes and focus exclusively on the indexes compiled for that particular nationality, port, group, or place. The best research strategy is the one that makes fullest use of your knowledge and saves you the most time and effort.

Following are four sample research scenarios that demonstrate how to utilize indexes to published passenger arrival information based on what you already know, or do not know, about your ancestor's immigration story. For each scenario, the title of a major work is provided to suggest the kind of index you would consult in that particular research situation. For complete publication data on all titles, refer to the bibliography. However, neither the bibliography nor the following examples are by any means exhaustive. They are illustrative only. You have to do your own research!

If All You Know Are the Three Basic Facts

Search for your ancestor's name in any index to published arrival records, such as this, the most extensive one available:

Filby, P. William, with Mary K. Meyer, eds. *Passenger and Immigration Lists Index: A Guide to Published Arrival Records of More Than 3,806,000 Passengers Who Came to the New World between the Sixteenth and the Early Twentieth Centuries.*

If You Also Know Your Ancestor's Nationality

Search for your ancestor's name in indexes to published arrival records compiled by nationality, such as:

Yoder, Don, ed. *Pennsylvania German Immigrants, 1709–1786: Lists Consolidated from Yearbooks of The Pennsylvania German Folklore Society.*

Mitchell, Brian, ed. *Irish Passenger Lists, 1803–1806.*

If You Also Know Your Ancestor's "Group" or Place of Settlement

Search for your ancestor's name in indexes to published arrival records compiled by religious or otherwise identifiable group, or by geographic place of settlement, such as:

Tepper, Michael H., ed. *Emigrants to Pennsylvania, 1641–1819: A Consolidation of Ship Passenger Lists from the Pennsylvania Magazine of History and Biography.*

Johnson, Amandus. *The Swedish Settlements on the Delaware, 1638–1664. 2 vols.*

If You Also Know Your Ancestor's Port of Arrival

Search for your ancestor's name in indexes to published arrival records that are compiled by port of arrival, such as:

Strassburger, Ralph Beaver, comp. *Pennsylvania German Pioneers: A Publication of the Original Lists of Arrivals in the Port of Philadelphia from 1727 to 1808.*

Taylor, Maureen A. *Rhode Island Passenger Lists: Port of Providence 1798–1808 and 1820–1872; Port of Bristol and Warren 1820–1871.*

When you find your ancestor's name in any of these indexes, you have completed step one of your search. Proceed to step two, using the reference cited in the index to locate the published arrival information. Often, as already stated, the transcribed or abstracted arrival information will be right there in the same volume with the index. When it is not, however, the index will indicate in what journal or book or article the information has been published. It will provide a title, author, and any other particulars necessary for you to identify the published work. Write down these bibliographical data and find a library that has a copy of the work.

Once you have the published work in hand, turn to the passenger list or other colonial document and read it line by line to find your ancestor's name. When you come to the name, be certain you have found your ancestor—and not someone else's of the same name—by double checking the data you find in the published record against what you already know to be your ancestor's full original name, approximate age at arrival, and approximate date of arrival. If they coincide, you have probably found a record of your ancestor's arrival in America, including, hopefully, the name of his or her ship.

Finally, to confirm that the information you have found pertains to your ancestor, you must bring to bear a corroborating fact—some piece of evidence found in the list itself or taken from outside information you know about your immigrant ancestor. For example, you know your ancestor Andrew Smith had a son James, and the Andrew Smith in the ship passenger list is enumerated with a wife and a son James. Or you know your ancestor Daniel O'Shea came to America with his brother Patrick, and the Daniel O'Shea in the list is written beside a Patrick O'Shea. The enormous number of immigrants with the same or similar names, and the scant information provided about each passenger in the old records, requires that you confirm your finding by bringing to bear at least one such corroborating fact.

Let us say, for example, that you are looking for the ship that brought your immigrant ancestor, William Bechet. The earliest record you have found for him is a Louisiana census of 1721, in which he appears as Guillaume Bechet, with a wife and a son, Jean. Guillaume is French for William, and you know your ancestor had a son, John, which in French is Jean. You hypothesize that Guillaume Bechet came within a few years of that census. Searching through Filby's *Passenger and Immigration Lists Index*, you find no Bechets at all in the original three-volume set, or the 1982–85 cumulative supplement. But in the 1986-90 cumulative supplement you find:

Bechet, Guillaume; Louisiana, 1719 **8421** p453
With wife

This looks promising. Checking the Sources Index in the front of the volume, you note that source 8421 is a series of two journal articles: "Ship Lists of Passengers Leaving France for Louisiana, 1718-1724," translated by Albert Laplace Dart, in *The Louisiana Historical*

Quarterly, volume 15, number 1 (January 1932), pages 68 through 77, and number 3 (July 1932), pages 453–467.

Visiting a library that has back issues of *The Louisiana Historical Quarterly*, you take volume fifteen and turn to page 453. There is the transcribed and translated passenger list of the flute *la Marie*, which sailed from France on 28 May 1719. (Types of ships, such as the flute, will be discussed later in this chapter.) The passenger list includes one *"Guillaume Bechet," "sa femme"* (his wife), and *"Jean Bechet agé de 4 ans"* (John Bechet, 4 years old). Though no age is given for Guillaume or his wife, and their relationship to the four-year-old boy is not indicated, the three passengers are grouped together, and that is sufficient confirmation that you have found your ancestor, because you know your *Guillaume Bechet* had a son John born about 1715.

This particular list is a record of *departure* from France, rather than a record of *arrival* in America. But in this case it serves the same purpose, since you know from the 1721 census of Louisiana that *la Marie* obviously did make it—the young Bechet family is there! Besides, no "arrival record," strictly speaking, is known to exist; this is as close as you will get, and it is a precious find indeed. Given the sailing date of 28 May 1719, it may be estimated confidently that the flute arrived sometime during the month of July. (Estimating the duration of a transatlantic crossing will be addressed in chapter 4.)

Your own research scenario may lead you to follow through on one, two, three, or all four of the sample strategies, or perhaps some combination of them. Or you may find it necessary to devise yet another strategy appropriate to your own research situation. Your course of action will depend on how much you know—or do not know—about the facts of your ancestor's immigration. Every piece you can fit into the puzzle will help complete the picture. Finding your immigrant ancestor's ship in this early period—1565 to 1819—often requires creative research methods. And a little luck does not hurt either!

Bibliography of Published Ship Passenger Lists

If you happen to know the name of your ancestor's ship, you may not need to consult any of the name indexes already described. Instead, you may turn immediately to an extensive bibliography of passenger arrival records that have appeared in *published* works and see whether your ancestor's ship appears there:

Filby, P. William. *Passenger and Immigration Lists Bibliography, 1538–1900: Being a Guide to Published Lists of Arrivals in the United States and Canada.*

This work lists hundreds of publications in which passenger arrival lists have appeared. Using the index in the back of the book, search for publications likely to contain your ancestor's ship list—that is, select works about your ancestor's place of arrival or place of settlement, or his or her ethnic, national, or religious group. Read the compiler's notes about each of those works to see which ships are named in them. If your ancestor's ship is mentioned, see whether the date of arrival coincides with your ancestor's approximate date of arrival. If it does not, the list is evidently from another crossing made by that ship, not your ancestor's crossing. Or it may be an entirely different ship that happened to have the same name as the one on which your ancestor sailed. If the date does fit, however, access the source cited, find the list in it, and search the list line by line for your forebear's name. When you find it, be sure to apply some corroborating piece of evidence to be sure you have found your ancestor and not someone else's!

For example, had you known that William Bechet arrived on the flute *la Marie*, you could have learned from Filby's *Passenger and Immigration Lists Bibliography* that at least one list of that vessel had been published—the list for a crossing made to Louisiana in 1719—

in *The Louisiana Historical Quarterly of 1932*. That would have provided sufficient incentive for you to access the issue and find your ancestor's name in the list.

Another helpful source to use when you already know the name of the sailing vessel that brought your forebear is an alphabetical listing of ships that carried immigrants to America. For example, David Dobson has authored *Ships from Ireland to Early America, 1623–1850*, and *Ships from Scotland to America, 1628–1828*. Books like these may facilitate your search by providing some precise dates of arrival, or some precise places of arrival, for your ancestor's ship. You could then look for passenger lists for those particular crossings, and perhaps find your ancestor's name on one of them.

If Your Ancestor Was a Slave

If your immigrant ancestor was an African transported to America in manacles, finding the ship will require a methodology completely distinct from the one already outlined. Slaves were not listed by name in any passenger list. Rather, they were logged in the slave ship's manifest as cargo, usually in age and sex categories. On occasion, slave manifests were more detailed, but usually only when ships were transporting slaves between domestic ports, not from Africa. Therefore, it is rarely possible to state categorically that you have found the ship on which your ancestor was brought to America in bondage.

Nevertheless, circumstantial evidence of your ancestor's ship *may* be obtained if you know where, when, and by whom the slave was first purchased, and then search through records pertaining to that place and time and slaveholder. It is not an easy task. On the contrary, it is difficult and time-consuming and requires advanced research skills. The materials you need to examine could be housed almost anywhere. Here are a few sample repositories:

National Archives

The National Archives has manifests of some ships importing slaves into the ports of Savannah, Mobile, and New Orleans during the period 1789-1808. They are part of Record Group 36 (Records  of the U.S. Customs Service) and may be examined in Washington, D.C. Since they contain no names, these lists have no index.

Museums

There are museums around the country that house special collections that include manifests of slave ships and private papers of slave owners. For example, the Peabody Essex Museum of Salem, Massachusetts, has some slave ship logbooks.

Libraries

Some libraries have published compilations of documents relating to the slave trade in America. These include official correspondence, proceedings, and reports of the officers of the shipping companies. One major work in this field is:

Donnan, Elizabeth, ed. *Documents Illustrative of the History of the Slave Trade in America.* 4 vols. Washington, D.C.: Carnegie Institution of Washington, 1930–35. Reprint by Octagon Books, New York, 1965.

For a list of archives, museums, and libraries that house major collections of value to Black American genealogy, see:

Burroughs, Tony. *Black Roots: A Beginner's Guide to Tracing the African American Family Tree*. New York: Simon & Schuster, 2001.

Also helpful is:

Streets, David H. *Slave Genealogy: A Research Guide with Case Studies*. Bowie, Md.: Heritage, 1986.

The search for a particular ship bringing manacled Africans to America, and the search for a particular ship carrying free Europeans or Asians, do share one unfortunate characteristic: success can never be guaranteed.

Learning More About Your Ancestor's Sailing Vessel

Once you discover the name of the sailing vessel that brought your ancestor to America, you may notice that it is preceded by the term "bark," "sloop," "snow," "brig," or some other designation, such as the

Drawing of a flute, a type of three-masted sailing vessel that brought many European immigrants to America in the 18th century. The row of cannons protruding through the hull show that this particular flute was armed for battle service. (From The Book of Old Ships by Henry B. Culver and Gordon Grant)

flute *la Marie* that carried the Bechet family. These terms indicate how the vessel was rigged, that is, the number of masts she had and the number and configuration of her sails. All of them were ships, so the generic term "ship" was often used instead of the more specific designation. If, however, the records do reveal what kind of ship your ancestors traveled in, it is not difficult to learn more about that type of vessel, and to obtain a reproduction of a drawing, painting, engraving or lithograph of one. Libraries are full of illustrated books about ships! Simply find a picture of a "bark" or "flute" or whatever other type of vessel your ancestor sailed in, dating from the era when your ancestor crossed the ocean, in a book such as Culver and Grant's *The Book of Old Ships*. As you make note of the rigging of such a ship, the shape of her hull, her size and weight, how many passengers she carried, and so forth, you will better appreciate your ancestor's immigration story. Larger ships with more sail could generally travel faster than lighter craft with less sail. Section VI of the bibliography at the end of this volume cites several books about sailing vessels, and Section VII suggests a few books that describe the experience of crossing the Atlantic under sail.

In addition, museums specializing in maritime history may be helpful in supplying information about, as well as a picture of, the type of vessel in which your ancestor sailed. (See chapter 5, "Obtaining a Picture of Your Ancestor's Ship," for more on this subject.)

Internet Websites

In addition to the sources and methods already discussed, the Internet, with its ever-multiplying websites, continues to provide new possibilities. Cyndi's List of Genealogy Sites on the Internet <www.cyndislist.com/ships.htm> links to numerous sites with information about ships, passenger lists, and crew lists. Sites are categorized under several headings, such as:

- libraries, archives & museums
- mailing lists, newsgroups & chat rooms
- professional researchers, volunteers & other research services
- publications, microfilm & microfiche
- shipwrecks
- societies & groups

Sites vary dramatically in quality and usefulness. Some are good, some are not. Most pertain to steamships rather than rigged vessels. Nevertheless, you cannot know what Internet website might be helpful in your quest for a forebear's ship until you investigate it. This is the place to begin your investigation.

For example, the Immigrant Ships Transcribers Guild <www.istg.rootsweb.com> is a group of volunteers who are transcribing passenger arrival records and up-loading them to the Internet. The selection of ships is still very small and selective, but it contains quite a few passenger lists of sailing vessels from the pre-1820 period, and it is easily searched. As is the case with most websites dealing with ships and passenger arrival records, random new material is uploaded at irregular intervals, and editorial direction and control are minimal. Always be a critical user of the Internet! Online search results are always "catch as catch can." Never accept as accurate any information you find online until you have double-checked it yourself against the source cited. If no source is cited, it is impossible to know whether the information is reliable or not.

As long as you are aware of its limitations, the ever-expanding amount of material appearing online warrants that you consult the Internet as you search for an immigrant ancestor's ship. (Much more about the Internet appears in chapter 4.)

Chapter Three

Passenger Lists
Since 1820

In 1819 Congress passed the Steerage Act, which required captains of
vessels arriving at U.S. ports from foreign countries to submit a list of
all passengers on board his ship to the Collector of Customs at the port
of entry. This act was signed into law and went into effect on 1 January.
This explains why the thousands of passenger lists at the National
Archives (with the few exceptions noted) date from 1820. These lists
are divided into two groups: Customs Passenger Lists (1820–ca. 1891)
and Immigration Passenger Lists (1891–1957).

Customs Passenger Lists (1820-ca. 1891)

Passenger lists dating from 1820 to about 1891 are called Customs
Manifests, or Customs Passenger Lists. The law stipulated that the list
give the name of the ship and her master, port of embarkation, date
and port of arrival, and each passenger's name, age, sex, occupation,
and nationality (See illustration). No more information than this was
required on Customs Passenger Lists, so many of them have only five
columns. Additional columns often recorded each passenger's berth
number and amount of baggage, as well as deaths at sea. The blank
lists were printed by private printers and sold to the ship companies
so they could fill them out and submit them in accordance with U.S.
law. Since there was no uniformity of size or appearance, the list format varies wildly.

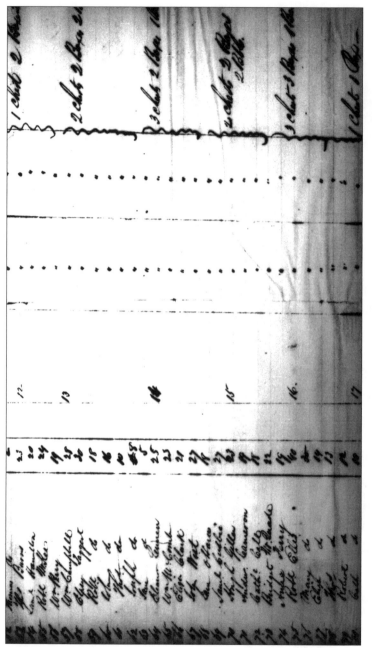

Customs Passenger List: This sample is from National Archives microfilm M425, Passenger Lists of Vessels Arriving at Philadelphia, 1800-1882, roll 53, Jan. 2-Dec. 24, 1838. It is the list of the bark Fairfield, arrived July 17, 1838, and it shows Robert Ellis and his family on lines 75 through 80.

Passenger Lists Since 1820

Given the scant amount of information provided in Customs Manifests, to be certain you have found your ancestor, you will want to have some corroborating evidence pertaining to your immigrant ancestor, learned from other sources. Customs Passenger Lists (part of Record Group 36, Records of the U.S. Customs Service) exist for the five major ports of Baltimore, Boston, New Orleans, New York, and Philadelphia, as well as numerous minor Atlantic, Gulf Coast, and Great Lakes ports.

How many American ports did immigrants use? In colonial times immigrants landed at hundreds of places along the rivers flowing into the Atlantic Ocean and Gulf of Mexico. No "immigrant receiving stations" enforced any physical, mental, or financial requirements for admission. As already noted, each colony or port city exercised authority over its own immigration affairs. The major port of entry during the eighteenth century was Philadelphia. However, with continued and increased immigration certain ports gradually became established points of arrival, and states assumed control of regulating immigration matters.

Throughout the nineteenth and into the early twentieth century, a total of 101 ports were used, and toward the end of the nineteenth century, "crossing stations" were established along the U.S. borders with Canada and Mexico, too. (For a complete, state-by-state listing of these ports and border-crossing stations, along with an account of the arrival records that exist for each one, the years the lists cover and their indexes, see chapter 2 of the *Guide to Genealogical Research in the National Archives*, or visit <www.nara.gov>.) There were five major ports—Boston, New York, Philadelphia, Baltimore, and New Orleans—and many minor ports, such as Portland, Maine; Gloucester, Mass.; New Haven, Conn.; Providence, R.I.; Wilmington, Del.; Norfolk, Va.; Savannah, Ga.; Charleston, S.C.; Key West, Fla.; Mobile, Ala.; and Galveston, Tex., among others.

Soon after the Erie Canal opened in 1825, New York City surpassed Philadelphia as the busiest port of entry. Getting into the interior of America was easier and cheaper than it had ever been, and immigration increased dramatically. It was during the 1830s that shipping companies started to realize the enormous profits to be made in transporting emigrants to America. All kinds of abuses developed, the worst of which was overcrowding, which fostered unhygienic conditions on board the ships. Disease and death were commonplace. To alleviate overcrowding, during the 1840s Congress passed a series of laws establishing tonnage-to-passenger ratios for ships arriving at U.S. ports.

In 1875 Congress asserted its prerogative to legislate immigration affairs by passing a law forbidding admission into the United States of criminals and women "brought for lewd and immoral purposes." The law was challenged and the case went all the way up to the Supreme Court, which upheld the federal government's jurisdiction over immigration matters. From 1875, therefore, the reception of immigrants arriving at all U.S. ports was handled jointly by federal and state officials. Though this shared federal/state system engendered tension and disputes, it lasted for fifteen years.

Congress passed a law in 1882 excluding from entry "any convict, lunatic, idiot or any person unable to take care of himself of herself without becoming a public charge." That same year, with passage of the "Chinese Exclusion Act," Congress barred—for the first time in American history—a particular national group from entering the country. (Certain categories of Chinese, such as students, businessmen and diplomats, continued to be allowed admittance for limited sojourns. For related information, see the section on "Lists of Chinese Passengers" in chapter 5.)

In 1890 the Secretary of the Treasury terminated the contract that his department held with the New York State Commissioners of Emigration, and the federal government assumed total control of immigration at the port of New York (for details, see the Conclusion, "A Word about Ellis Island"). The following year the joint federal/state system was terminated in all other U.S. ports. The 1891 law also provided for the creation of immigrant receiving stations at U.S. ports, and stipulated that henceforth steamship companies would be responsible for carrying back to their homelands all passengers refused admittance by federal government inspectors at the receiving stations.

It was then, in 1891, that a separate bureau with its own head was created for handling immigration affairs, another "first" in American history. This was the Office of Immigration, carved out of the Department of the Treasury; its head was called the Superintendent of Immigration.

Immigration Passenger Lists (1891-1957)

Passenger lists dating from 1891 to 1957 are called Immigration Manifests, or Immigration Passenger Lists, because collecting and retaining them was now the responsibility of the new U.S. Office of Immigration. Standard forms for recording the required information about passengers arriving in the United States came into use in 1893. Their size, color, and quality of paper were specified in detail by law, but it was still the responsibility of the individual steamship companies to obtain their own manifests. They kept a supply in their respective ports of embarkation around the world to be filled in by an officer and submitted upon arrival in the U.S. port. Over the years, the collection and maintenance of the completed lists shifted from the Department of the Treasury, first to the Department of Commerce and Labor, then to the Department of Justice, and finally in 1906 to the newly created Immigration and Naturalization Service. (The current disposition of the lists is explained in a later section.)

39

The amount of information about each passenger required in an Immigration Manifest expanded dramatically in the late nineteenth and early twentieth centuries (See illustration). While the vast majority of immigrants prior to 1882 had come from Northern and Western Europe and had been predominantly Protestant, by 1907 three out of every four immigrants were Catholics and Jews from Southern and Eastern Europe. The U.S. government wanted to know more about these millions of "New Immigrants" flocking to its shores, so Congress could effectively legislate immigration matters. Following is a summary of the data Congress required for each passenger over the years.

1893

In 1893 the number of columns was increased from the five of the Customs Passenger Lists to twenty-one. In addition to each passenger's name, age, sex, occupation, and nationality, passengers were asked to give the following information:

- marital status
- last residence
- final destination in the United States
- if ever in the United States before, when, where, and for how long
- if going to join a relative, the relative's name, address and relationship
- whether able to read and write
- whether in possession of a train ticket to his or her final destination
- who paid the passage
- amount of money the passenger was carrying
- whether the passenger had ever been in a prison, almshouse,

or institution for the insane, or was a polygamist
* state of health

Note that each passenger's "last residence" was now recorded, not just his or her nationality or country of origin. Since most emigrants, prior to emigrating, resided in the village or town or city of their birth, this column may provide the name of the ancestor's birthplace. At the very least, it leads the way to continued research in your ancestor's native land.

Column fourteen, "Whether in possession of money, [and if so] if so, whether more than $30 and how much if $30 or less," resulted from the 1882 law requiring that arriving immigrants not become public charges. The minimum acceptable amount became set unofficially at $20; immigrants in possession of less than that were not admitted. Word spread among the towns and villages of Europe that $20 was sufficient to get into the United States, so rarely did arriving passengers declare more than that amount. Often they carried their entire life's savings sewn into the linings of their coats and the hems of their skirts—but they had no intention of telling that to a government official wearing a uniform!

The outbreak of cholera in Europe in 1893, followed by a period of economic depression in the United States that did not end until 1897, discouraged immigration during those years. From 1898, however, immigration resumed in ever increasing numbers.

1903

By the Immigration Act of 1903, Congress added a twenty-second column to ship passenger lists to allow the federal government to keep a statistical account of the ethnic groups migrating to the shores of America:

* Race or People

Immigration Passenger List. This list is from National Archives microfilm T715, Passenger and Crew Lists of Vessels Arriving at New York 1897-1957, roll 1095, "Volumes 2404-2405, April 20, 1908." It is the list of the SS. Florida, arrived 20 April 1908, and it shows Salvatore Piraino on line 15.

STATES IMMIGRATION OFFICER AT PORT OF ARRIVAL.

to the United States Immigration Officer by the Commanding Officer of any vessel having such passengers on board upon arrival before a port in the United States.

Arriving at Port of **NEW-YORK** April the 20th ——— , 190 ——

13	14	15	16	17	18	19	20	21	22	23	24	25	26			27	28	29	

European empires, and many smaller nations throughout the world, included peoples of a variety of ethnic backgrounds. For example, an ancestor from "Austria-Hungary" could have been Austrian, German, Hungarian, Ukrainian, Czech, Slovak, Bohemian, Moravian, Croatian, Slovenian, Serbian, Polish, or perhaps even Italian. This new column, therefore, may help you localize your research on your immigrant ancestor's family overseas.

1906

In 1906, six more columns were added:

- personal description, including height, complexion, color of hair, color of eyes, and identifying marks
- place of birth

Note that now—for the first time—passenger lists provided the *exact* city, town, or village where each passenger was born—not just his or her race or people, last residence, or nationality. This valuable information leads you *directly* to the birthplace of your immigrant ancestor.

It was also in 1906 that the United States signed a "Gentleman's Agreement" with the emperor of Japan. In it, the emperor agreed that he would no longer allow his subjects to emigrate to the United States.

1907

In 1907 an additional column was included on ship passenger lists, bringing the total number of columns to twenty-nine:

- name and address of closest living relative in native country

Births and Deaths at Sea, Stowaways, and Other Information

Though not required by law, many Customs Passenger Lists included a separate column for recording deaths that occurred while the vessel was crossing to North America. On lists not having such a column, information about deaths at sea, as well as births at sea, was added at the end of the list as the events happened. For example, the last line of the passenger list of the ship *Neptune*, arriving in New York from Liverpool on 2 September 1865, reads "Infant Spann Born Aug. 29 see No 385," and at passenger number 385 (just below "John Spann, 49, male, servant, Ireland") appears "Mary Ann do, 30, female, servant, Ireland" with the inserted notation "Infant born aug. 29th." The last five lines of the passenger list of the ship *American Union*, which sailed into New York from Liverpool on 16 August 1865, bears witness to a particularly tragic crossing:

Deaths

189 Costello Thomas 12 months 28th July 1865
454 McNulty Patrick 8   "   2nd   "
589 Buesly Albert 13   "   27th   "
314 Moorehouse Charles 14   "   2nd Aug.   "
327 Joseph Campbell 2 years   7th   "

Inserted at each child's entry in the passenger list is a notation of his death, with date. The transatlantic voyage seems to have been hardest on the little ones.

The names of stowaways discovered at sea, or when the vessel docked, were also added to the end of the list. For example, the SS. *Round Brook*, pulling into Boston Harbor from Barbados on 13 October 1905, had on board one "Isaac Williams, 32, black, stowaway." It is also possible that the stowaway's name might appear on the ship's crew list, because stowaways discovered en route were often impressed into service to earn their passage to America (more about crew lists in chapter 5). Stowaways who succeeded in remaining undetected were, of course, never recorded on any list, passenger or crew.

To many twentieth-century Immigration Passenger Lists a second list—titled "Record of Aliens Held for Special Inquiry"—was appended after the ship had docked and the passengers had been inspected by U.S. officials. This supplemental list contains the names of all passengers who were detained for any reason. It may note, for instance, that a passenger arrived with measles and had to spend three weeks in the infirmary of the immigrant receiving station before being admitted to the United States. A passenger who did not possess the minimum amount of cash required for admittance would be noted as "l.p.c."—likely public charge—and detained until the necessary funds arrived from a relative or friend in the United States. Passengers denied admittance to the United States because of glaucoma or some other medical condition are named with the date of their deportation. An unmarried woman traveling alone, especially a young one, was sometimes detained until a male relative or fiancé came to the immigrant facility to escort her (in the case of a fiancé, *after* marrying her, of course!) to her U.S. destination. These lists of detainees were microfilmed together with the original ship passenger lists to which they belong.

Many Immigration Passenger Lists also bear handwritten notations made by the American officials who inspected the arriving passengers. For instance, depending on the year and the immigration laws in effect at the time, a naturalized U.S. citizen who went back to his native land and then returned with a wife and children could be required to prove his American citizenship before being allowed to re-enter the country with his family. If the foreign-born citizen did not have his citizenship certificate with him, immigration officials would wire the court where the naturalization had taken place for the required confirmation. The results of this inquest would be hastily penned on the naturalized American's line in the passenger list—providing the family historian with a direct lead to the immigrant ancestor's naturalization record!

The U.S. officials who questioned the immigrants also made corrections on the lists when an immigrant's response varied from the information originally recorded on the list in the port of embarkation.

Many steamships coming to the United States in the nineteenth and twentieth centuries boarded passengers not only at the initial port of embarkation, but at one or two intermediate ports as well. A ship sailing from Hamburg, Germany, for instance, might board additional passengers at Liverpool, England, and Cherbourg, France, on her way to Boston. This is why, as you search through a passenger list, you may find different ports of embarkation given on different pages of the list. This could also explain why you find your English ancestor coming to America on a German ship out of Hamburg. (Chapter 4 contains more about this topic under "Emigration Lists.")

There are Immigration Passenger Lists (part of Record Group 85, Records of the Immigration and Naturalization Service) for the five major ports of Baltimore, Boston, New Orleans, New York, and Philadelphia; for the minor ports of Detroit (Mich.), Key West (Fla.), Galveston (Tex.), Gloucester and New Bedford (Mass.); Portland (Maine), Providence (R.I.), San Francisco (Calif.), Port Townsend, Tacoma, and Seattle (Wash.), Skagway and Eagle (Alaska), as well as for ports in Alabama, Florida, Georgia, and South Carolina. (Once again, for full details, consult the *Guide to Genealogical Research at the National Archives*, or visit <www.nara.gov>.)

The original Customs Passenger Lists and Immigration Passenger Lists are no longer stored at the National Archives. They were all microfilmed (except as noted), mostly during 1943–44. After the microfilming, the Customs Passenger Lists from the five major ports were given to Temple University. Today they are housed in that institution's Balch Institute for Ethnic Studies, 18 South Seventh St., Philadelphia, PA 19106 (See <www.balchinstitute.org> for further details and excellent information). The Immigration Passenger Lists, however, were destroyed in 1948 after being microfilmed. All lists at the National Archives are on microfilm.

Does the National Archives have a microfilm copy of the passenger list of *every* ship that arrived in *every* U.S. port between 1820 and 1957? No! First of all, most ports did not serve as entry points for immigrants for the entire 1820-1957 period; rather, they served that purpose for much more limited spans of years. Furthermore, many lists are known to be missing: Galveston lists of 1872 through 1895, for instance, are nonexistent; and there is a half-year gap from January through June 1833 in the lists for New Orleans; and the lists for Charleston cover only 1820 through 1829. Finally, due to a change in I.N.S. microfilming procedure in the late 1940s, quite a few passenger lists for thirteen ports were destroyed without being preserved on microfilm; these records covered arrivals during various periods between 1948 and 1954. Some authorities say the National Archives may lack up to ten percent of the total number of passenger lists created. Others suggest that up to forty percent may be lacking, though that figure would appear to be grossly exaggerated. In truth, however, no one knows for sure. What is certain is that thousands upon thousands of lists have survived the ravages of time and are available on microfilm at the National Archives for your inspection!

The Customs Passenger Lists and Immigration Passenger Lists at the National Archives are arranged by port of arrival, and thereunder chronologically. Each port is given a micropublication number and a title, and may include from one to over 6,000 rolls of microfilm which are all labeled by date and number. For example, *Passenger Lists of*

Passenger Lists Since 1820

Vessels Arriving at Boston, Mass., *1820–1891* is micropublication M277 and contains 115 rolls. Roll number one contains lists from 22 September 1820 to 30 March 1825; roll number two contains lists from 4 April 1825 to 30 June 1826; and so forth. *Passenger Lists of Vessels Arriving at Boston, Mass.*, *1891–1943* is micropublication T843 and comprises 454 rolls. Roll number one contains lists for 1891; roll number two contains lists for 1892; and so on. These many thousands of rolls of microfilmed passenger lists are kept in file cabinets in National Archives stacks adjacent to Room 400, the Microfilm Reading Room at the National Archives. The LDS Family History Library has copies of all of them, which means they may be borrowed and viewed at any LDS Family History Center worldwide. In addition, major public libraries around the country also have copies of these National Archives micropublications.

Some Peculiarities of the Passenger Arrival Records

To use these voluminous passenger arrival records most effectively, it may be useful to know something about how the National Archives microfilm publications were assembled. Each port has its own peculiarities. First of all, you should be aware that the "lists" you see on the microfilm are not always the original passenger lists submitted upon arrival in the U.S. port. Many are copies.

The law of 1819 referred to previously mandated the creation of passenger arrival lists for the Customs Bureau. It further mandated that the Customs Bureau prepare copies of the lists they collected at U.S. ports for the State Department on a quarterly basis. To fulfill this mandate, some customs collectors made copies of the individual lists, while other customs collectors created "abstracts"; that is, they consolidated into a single list the names of all passengers who arrived during the entire quarter. These copies and abstracts were submitted to the State Department between 1820 and 1874, when the practice was abandoned.

From these quarterly copies and abstracts, State Department officials prepared annual statistical reports on immigration, which they submitted to Congress along with transcripts of the lists. But the lists grew more numerous each year, and transcribing them required more and more time. It was probably decided that the statistical reports alone would suffice for Congress to legislate immigration matters, because transcripts prepared by the State Department for Congress were only submitted between 1820 and 1832, and then the practice was discontinued. Those that were created between 1820 and 1832 comprise nine volumes, although volume two, unfortunately, has been missing for many years. (Volume one actually contains some arrivals during October, November, and December 1819.) The eight extant volumes have been microfilmed as T1219, *State Department Transcripts of Passenger Lists, ca. October 1819–ca. December 1832* (2 rolls).

When federal officials were microfilming and indexing the passenger arrival records, they wanted to compile as complete a record as possible for each port. This could be achieved only by "filling in" the periodic gaps in the *original* lists with these *derivative lists*. (See Michael Tepper's *American Passenger Arrival Records* for a thorough explanation of how the "lists" for each port were assembled.) What is significant for family researchers is that derivatives are generally distinguishable from originals in this way: the U.S. government copyists often used only *initials* rather than the full given names of the passengers, and omitted information they considered extraneous to their purpose. They were preparing *abstracts* of the original lists, not verbatim *copies*.

Sometimes the quarterly abstracts prepared by the Customs Bureau for the State Department were microfilmed as a separate publication. For example, *Passenger Lists of Vessels Arriving at Baltimore, MD, 1820–1891* is M255 (fifty rolls), while *Quarterly Abstracts of*

Passenger Lists of Vessels Arriving at Baltimore, MD, 1820–1869 is M596 (six rolls). Comparing the two records for a single passenger reveals that the information given in the abstract is an abbreviated version of the information given in the original list. Furthermore, some of the passenger arrival lists used by government officials to "fill in the gaps" are not even federal records. They are state or local records. The following sample ports will show why this is significant.

Boston

All of the original Customs Passenger Lists for Boston prior to 1883 were destroyed by fire, so State Department copies and transcripts were used in place of the missing originals. These derivative records are what you see on micropublication M277, *Passenger Lists of Vessels Arriving at Boston, MA, 1820–1891*. But these copies and abstracts covered only 22 September 1820 through 31 March 1874. For the period of 1 April 1874 through 31 December 1882, no federal arrival records of any kind—original or derivative—survived. So micropublication M277 has an eight-and-a-half-year gap on roll 87. Fortunately for family historians researching Boston immigrants, passenger arrival records created in accordance with a Massachusetts state law of 1848 serve to fill in that gap! But those lists are not on microfilm in the National Archives collection. They are available only at the Massachusetts State Archives, 220 Morrissey Blvd., Boston, MA 02125 (See <http://www.state. ma.us/sec/arc/arcidx.htm> for further information).

Oddly, the passengers enumerated on those state lists are included in the National Archives index to Boston arrivals, micropublication M625! So if you discover a card in M625 for an ancestor arriving between 1 April 1874 and 31 December 1882, you must then write to the Massachusetts Archives for a photocopy of the relevant page of the passenger list.

Baltimore

From 1833 through 1866, a Maryland state law required the masters of vessels arriving in Baltimore to submit a list of passengers on board to the mayor of the city. When the arrival records for Baltimore were compiled and microfilmed, these "city lists" came in very handy for filling in the sporatic gaps that existed in the federal lists. When you use National Archives micropublication M255, *Passenger Lists of Vessels Arriving at Baltimore, MD, 1820–1891*, any list you examine between 1833 and 1866 may be a federal record or a Maryland state record.

This explains why there are two separate indexes to Baltimore arrival records: one (M327) covering passengers named in the federal lists, and another (M326) covering passengers named in the city lists. So, when looking for a Baltimore arrival of 1833 to 1866, you will want to search both indexes, because you have no way of knowing whether your ancestor's record has survived on a federal list or a city list.

Philadelphia

Passenger arrival records for Philadelphia begin, not in 1820, but in 1800. Even before the federal legislation of 1819, an earlier act of Congress had exempted incoming passengers from paying duty on a limited amount of personal baggage. Authorities at the port of Philadelphia, ever scrupulous in their record-keeping, maintained lists of names of arriving passengers whose personal baggage exceeded that limit and was, therefore, subject to taxation. These were called "Baggage Lists." Although the original Baggage Lists are not kept at the National Archives (they are in the Pennsylvania State Archives in Harrisburg), they were included in micropublication M425, *Passenger Lists of Vessels Arriving at Philadelphia, PA, 1800–1882*, to make the passenger arrival records as complete as possible for Philadelphia.

The Baggage Lists are included in National Archives micropublication M360, *Index to Passenger Lists of Vessels Arriving at Philadelphia, PA,*

1800–1906. Of course, the names of passengers whose personal baggage did not exceed the duty-free limit would not appear in these lists.

Galveston

For the port of Galveston, there are no arrival records at all, federal or state, for the period 1872 through 1895, inclusive. Galveston arrivals from 1846 through 1871 are available on micropublication M575, roll 3 (although these are quarterly abstracts and many quarters are missing), and Galveston arrivals from 1896 to 1951 are on micropublication M1359 (which does include a few scattered lists from 1892 and 1893 as well). Except for those few scattered lists, a wide gap of 1872 through 1895 remains.

This may not represent as devastating a loss of arrival records as it would appear at first glance, however. The great majority of immigrant ships arriving in Galveston during the latter half of the nineteenth century sailed from Bremen, Germany, and departure statistics for that port show that no emigrant vessels left for Galveston from July 1875 through June 1880, and from July 1887 through June 1896. This fact reduces the period of missing lists—for Bremen arrivals, at least—down dramatically to July 1880 through June 1887. Nevertheless, it is still an unfortunate gap in Galveston passenger arrival records. (For further details, see the article by Lawrence H. Konecny cited in the bibliography.)

New Orleans

During the 1930s, the Work Progress Administration of Louisiana prepared six typewritten volumes titled, *Passenger Lists Taken From Manifests of the Customs Service, Port of New Orleans.* These books—minus Volume 5, which is missing—are in the library of the National Archives in Washington, D.C. Volumes 1, 2, and 3 have been microfilmed as M2009, *Works Progress Administration Transcript of Passenger*

Lists of Vessels Arriving at New Orleans, Louisiana, 1813–1849 (2 rolls). Volumes 4 and 6 have not been microfilmed. Each volume includes an alphabetical name index to the passengers listed.

The passenger arrival records of Boston, Baltimore, Philadelphia, Galveston, and New Orleans serve to demonstrate the kinds of peculiarities you will encounter from port to port and year to year. The more you work with these micropublications, the more peculiarities you are likely to notice. You will want to take them into consideration as you search for your ancestors' ships.

National Archives Indexes

So how do you find one passenger among the millions in all of these rolls of passenger lists? By using indexes! (Some of these have already been mentioned.) Fortunately for family historians, one of the undertakings of the Work Projects Administration (WPA) during the Depression was composing personal name indexes to ship passenger lists for the Immigration and Naturalization Service.

Reading through the lists line by line, indexers created a three-by-five index card for each passenger (See illustration). Sufficient information was handwritten or typed onto each card to allow future researchers to identify a particular passenger and find him or her in the ship list. This information usually included the passenger's name, age, sex, occupation, country of origin, port of departure, name of the ship, and her date and port of arrival. The completed indexes were then microfilmed and the original three-by-five cards were destroyed (with rare exceptions—see Tepper's *American Passenger Arrival Records*).

These microfilmed indexes—available at the National Archives, the thirteen Regional Archives, thousands of LDS Family History Centers worldwide (by borrowing from the Family History Library in Salt Lake City), and many larger public libraries—make searching for

Alphabetical Index Card. This sample is from National Archives microfilm M360, Index to Passenger Lists of Vessels Arriving at Philadelphia, 1800-1906, roll 40, "Ellis, H.-Es." It shows that Robert Ellis arrived 17 July 1838 on the bark Fairfield.

a particular passenger a feasible undertaking. Unfortunately, the WPA workers did not complete an index for every port for every year. The indexes to passenger arrivals at the five major ports and the periods they cover are as follows:

- Baltimore: 1820–1897, 1833–1866 and 1897–1952
- Boston: 1848–1891, 1902–1906 and 1906–1920
- New Orleans: 1853–1899 and 1900–1952
- New York: 1820–1846, 1897–1902, 1902–1943 and 1944–1948
- Philadelphia: 1800–1906 and 1883–1948

Note that many of the peak years of immigration into Boston—1892 through 1901—and into New York—1847 through 1896—are not included in these National Archives indexes. But do not despair! There are many other indexes and resources discussed in chapter 4 to help you search those years. First, however, let's consider in some detail what these National Archives indexes on microfilm are and how to use them.

Some peculiarities of the indexes to passenger arrivals at Boston (M625), Baltimore (M325 and M326), and Philadelphia (M360) have already been pointed out. But note, too, that the two indexes to Philadelphia arrivals overlap for the years 1883 through 1906. You may use either index (or both, to be most thorough) to find a passenger arriving in Philadelphia during that span of years.

There are also indexes to passengers arriving at many minor ports:

- Atlantic, Gulf Coast, and Great Lakes ports: 1820–1874
- Alabama, Florida, Georgia, and South Carolina ports: 1890–1924
- Detroit, Mich.: 1906–1954
- Eagle, Hyder, Ketchikan, Nome, and Skagway, Alaska: 1906-1946
- Galveston, Tex.: 1896–1906 and 1906–1951
- Gulfport, Miss.: 1904–1954
- Pascagoula, Miss.: 1903–1935
- New Bedford, Mass.: 1902–1954
- Portland, Maine: 1893–1954
- Providence, R.I.: 1911–1954
- San Diego, Calif.: ca. 1904–ca. 1952
- San Francisco, Calif.: 1893–1934
- Tampa, Fla.: 1898–1945

Each of these indexes has an identifying number as well as title, and may comprise from one to over 700 rolls of microfilm. Each roll is labeled. For example, *Index to Passengers Arriving at New Bedford, Mass., July 1, 1902–November 18, 1954* is micropublication T522 and comprises two rolls. Roll one is labeled, "Abalo-Simas, Marie Da," and roll two is labeled, "Simas, Maria Da-Zuzarte." All of these indexes are kept in file drawers near the microfilmed ship passenger lists in the National Archives.

A Supplemental Index to . . . Atlantic and Gulf Coast Ports

One index in particular must be highlighted here because its contents are often misunderstood. This index, called *A Supplemental Index to Passenger Lists of Vessels Arriving at Atlantic and Gulf Coast Ports (Excluding New York), 1820–1874* (micropublication M334), covers passengers arriving at 71 of the 101 ports in use in the nineteenth century. This includes 67 minor ports such as Portland (Maine), Wilmington (Del.), and Charleston (S.C.) on the Atlantic; Galveston (Tex.) and Mobile (Ala.) on the Gulf Coast; and Rochester (N.Y.) and Sandusky (Ohio) on the Great Lakes. The passenger lists of the 67 minor ports included in the *Supplemental Index* are contained on micropublication M575, *Copies of Lists of Passengers Arriving at Miscellaneous Ports on the Atlantic and Gulf Coasts and at Ports on the Great Lakes, 1820–1873.* However, it is important to note that the *Supplemental Index* also covers some passengers arriving at four of the five major ports as well! New York City is the only major port not included in the *Supplemental Index.*

Therefore, if your ancestor came to any port, minor or major, other than New York, between 1820 and 1874, your search of National Archives indexes is not exhaustive until you have examined the *Supplemental Index.* This is particularly significant for Boston and New Orleans arrivals, because the *Index to Passenger Lists of Vessels Arriving at Boston* (M265) does not begin until 1848, and the *Index to Passenger Lists of Vessels Arriving at New Orleans* (T527) does not begin until 1853. But the *Supplemental Index* does include some Boston arrivals

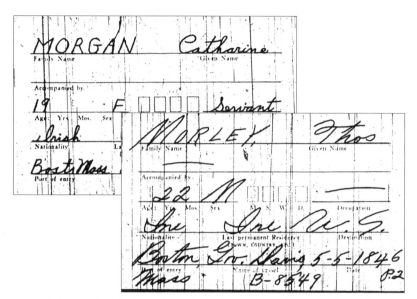

Two cards from National Archives micropublication M334, A Supplemental Index to Passenger Lists of Vessels Arriving at Atlantic and Gulf Coast Ports [Excluding New York], 1820-1874, show that it includes some pre-1848 Boston arrivals, thus supplementing the Index to Passenger Lists of Vessels Arriving at Boston, MA, 1848-1891, M265.

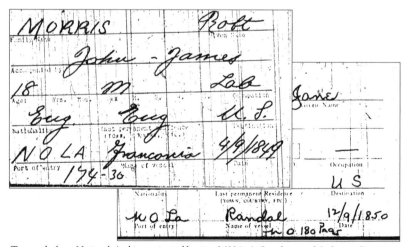

Two cards from National Archives micropublication M334, A Supplemental Index to Passenger Lists of Vessels Arriving at Atlantic and Gulf Coast Ports [Excluding New York], 1820-1874, show that this index includes some pre-1853 New Orleans arrivals, thus supplementing the Index to Passenger Lists of Vessels Arriving at New Orleans, LA, 1853-1899, T527.

between 1820 and 1847, and some New Orleans arrivals between 1820 and 1852.

All of the National Archives indexes are one of two different kinds: those in which the passengers' surnames are listed in alphabetical order, and those in which the surnames are listed according to the Soundex indexing system. Following are two sample research cases to illustrate how these indexes work.

Alphabetical Indexes

Let's say you know the three basic facts about your immigrant ancestor: his name is Ignazio Colletta; he arrived in America about 1890; and he was about thirty-six years old at the time. In addition, oral family tradition claims that Ignazio came to work on the railroads and that he laid track in the far West for several years. You are ready to begin your search.

The first thing you must do, by process of elimination, is learn his port of arrival. To do this, you search for Ignazio Colletta in every index that covers 1890 arrivals.

To be thorough, always search a year or two on either side of the supposed year of arrival, and always search under all possible variant spellings of the surname and given name. In the case of Ignazio Colletta, consider that he may have arrived in 1888, 1889, 1890, 1891, or 1892, that he may have been 34, 35, 36, 37, or 38 years old, and that his

Immigrant Experience. Thousands of poor European men, such as Ignazio Colletta (shown here with his wife, Rosalia Geraci), streamed to the United States in the 1890s to fill industry's demand for labor, and then returned home. Many came several times, crossing the Atlantic four, six or even eight times; steamships made it possible. Wives tended "the home front" while husbands labored in America. Ignazio Colletta came with nine buddies in 1890 on board the SS. Trinacria to lay track out West; he went home in 1894.

name may appear in the list as Colletta, or Colleta, or Coletta, etc. This way, you won't miss any likely candidates.

You search the Baltimore, Boston, and Philadelphia indexes without finding a single passenger who fits the facts for your ancestor. The last index to turn to is the one for New Orleans, since New York arrivals are not indexed for 1890. If you do not find Ignazio Colletta in the New Orleans index, you will assume he arrived at the port of New York and continue your search for his ship using the other resources and strategies discussed in chapter 4.

The index to passenger arrivals at New Orleans is in two parts. *Index to Passenger Lists of Vessels Arriving at New Orleans, La., 1853–1899*, is an alphabetical index, microfilm T527 (32 rolls). *Index to Passenger Lists of Vessels Arriving at New Orleans, La., 1900–1952*, is also an alphabetical index, microfilm T618 (22 rolls). Since you know Ignazio Colletta arrived about 1890, you are going to use microfilm T527.

Roll number six is labeled "Claude, Joseph-Dallu, L." You take it from the file drawer and crank it through the microfilm reader until you come to a card bearing the surname "Coleta." A quick glance confirms that there is a string of cards for Coleta, Coletta, Colleta, and Colletta passengers. Familiar now with how the lists were created, you realize that any spelling could be your ancestor. You find only one "Ignazio," an "Ignazio Coletta." You have completed step one of the research process!

The microfilmed index card contains a number of boxes into which the indexer has transcribed from the original passenger list certain facts about the passenger. He is a thirty-six-year-old male laborer from Italy and appears in the list of the SS. *Trinacria*, which sailed from Palermo, Sicily, and arrived in New Orleans on 9 June 1890. Could he be your ancestor? You must examine the list to know for sure. So you proceed to step two of the research process: use the information given on the index card to locate "Ignazio Coletta" in the list of the SS. *Trinacria*.

SS. Trinacria. *Note how this steamship is fully rigged to take advantage of a good wind, if one comes along. Courtesy of Peabody Essex Museum of Salem.*

You return roll number six of microfilm T527 to its drawer. (Be careful to replace the microfilm exactly where you found it!) Then you take a few steps to the file drawers containing *Passenger Lists of Vessels Arriving at New Orleans, La., 1820–1902,* microfilm M259 (ninety-three rolls). Roll number seventy-three is labeled "Oct. 2, 1889–June 25, 1890." You take it and crank it through the reader until you come to the list of the SS. *Trinacria.* Now you search the passenger list line by line until you find "Ignazio Coletta." There he is!

His first name, age, and year of arrival all fit your ancestor perfectly, but his surname appears with only one "l." You will want to check a few additional facts in the passenger list to confirm that this man is indeed your ancestor. First, this "Ignazio Coletta" sailed from Palermo, Sicily, and you know that your ancestor was Sicilian, and that Palermo would be his closest port. That fits. Second, you recognize the surnames of the four young men enumerated in the list just above Ignazio, and the five young men enumerated just below him, as those of families of your ancestor's village. Obviously, they were ten *paesani*, or neighbors, traveling together. This confirms the family tradition that

Ignazio came to work on the railroads, since agents for the railroad companies would travel through Europe rounding up laborers, then ship them together to America. So that fits, too.

Using an alphabetical index to ship passenger lists is not difficult. But be alert to any evidence in the list that confirms the passenger you have found is indeed your own ancestor, and not someone else's with the same name!

Soundex Indexes

The indexes that are not alphabetical are Soundex. The Soundex system was developed for the National Archives by Remington Rand Corporation in the 1930s as a means of creating personal name indexes to records according to the sounds of the names rather than their actual spellings. The initial letter of each name is retained, the subsequent consonants are assigned numbers, and the vowels are ignored. The name Schmitt, for example, appears under the Soundex category of S-530, along with Smith and Schumad and Sheeneth and a variety of other names that all begin with the letter "S" and have the same subsequent consonant sounds.

Within each Soundex code, the names are alphabetized under the first letter of the *first* name. Under S-530, for example, "Schmitt, Johann" would follow "Smith, Andrew." "Sheeneth, Donald," would fall between "Smith, Andrew" and "Schmitt, Johann."

Within each group of same *first* names, individuals are listed by order of age, from youngest to oldest. A Donald who is twelve years of age would be listed in the index before a Donald who is forty-three.

There are special rules for coding surnames beginning with prefixes—such as "Di Giovanni," "Van Camp" and "De LaFayette"—as well as surnames containing consonant blends and double consonants. An explanation of how to use the Soundex system appears in every National Archives publication. See, for example, "Guide to the

Soundex Index Card. *This card is from National Archives microfilm T621, Index (SOUNDEX) to Passenger Lists of Vessels Arriving at New York, July 1, 1902-Dec. 31, 1943, roll 551, P-650 Armando-P-652 Marian M. It shows that Salvatore Piraino arrived 20 April 1908, on the SS. Florida.*

Soundex System," page 163 of *Immigrant and Passenger Arrivals*. A "Soundex converter" may also be accessed at <www.nara.gov>.

The cards in the Soundex indexes are similar to those found in the alphabetical indexes (See illustration). They contain a number of boxes which the WPA indexer used to transcribe from the list various data about the passenger, including name, age, sex, occupation, country of origin, port of embarkation, and, of course, the name of the ship and the date and port of her arrival.

Let us say you are looking for Domenico Geraci. You know he came to the United States around 1911 at about the age of forty-six, so you have the three basic facts needed to begin a search. Additionally, your research has revealed that Domenico had a wife whose name was Rosalia Marrone; this "identifying fact" may prove useful. You do not know Domenico's port of arrival, but decide to begin your search with New York, since that port is a likely possibility for an Italian immigrant arriving about 1911, and it is indexed for that year. (For a word about determining an ancestor's most likely port of arrival, see "Determining

Your Ancestor's Probable Port of Departure" in chapter 4.) If you do not find Domenico Geraci in the New York index, you will proceed to search the indexes to other ports. Once again, it is the process of elimination that will lead you to his port.

The index to passenger arrivals at New York is in four parts. *Index to Passenger Lists of Vessels Arriving at New York, N.Y., 1820–1846*, is an alphabetical index, micropublication M261 (103 rolls). *Index to Passenger Lists of Vessels Arriving at New York, N.Y., June 16, 1897–June 30, 1902* is also an alphabetical index, micropublication T519 (115 rolls). But *Index (SOUNDEX) to Passenger Lists of Vessels Arriving at New York, N.Y., July 1, 1902–December 31, 1943*, is a Soundex index, micropublication T621 (755 rolls). And *Index (SOUNDEX) to Passenger Lists of Vessels Arriving at the Port of New York, 1944-48* is also a Soundex index, micropublication M1417 (ninety-four rolls).

Since Domenico Geraci arrived about 1911, you are going to use microfilm T621. This means you will have to translate the name *Geraci* into the Soundex code. You come up with G-620. Roll number 244 is labeled "G-620 Caroline—G-620 Johann." You take it from the drawer and crank it through all the first names beginning with C and D until you find the following sequence of index cards:

Gorga, Domenico ... 44 years old, etc.
Grasso, Domenico ... 45 years old, etc.
Greco, Domenico ... 46 years old, etc.
Geraci, Domenico ... 46 years old, etc.

You have found a forty-six-year-old Domenico Geraci who arrived at the port of New York. Step one of the research process is accomplished. But is he your ancestor? You need to examine the passenger list. So proceed to step two: use the information given on the index card to find Domenico Geraci in the passenger list. As the case of Ignazio Colletta just demonstrated, it is a simple matter of using the data from the index card to locate the passenger list and find your ancestor in it—with one exception.

Post-1910 New York Arrivals

The exception applies to passenger arrivals at the port of New York only, after 1910 only, because a different index card was used. This index card gives much less information about the passenger, and this limited information is given in a simplified, numerical fashion. It is obvious from the appearance of Domenico Geraci's index card that he arrived after 1910. It looks like this:

GERACI, Domenico 46m 3 13 3942

This means that Domenico Geraci is a forty-six-year-old male and that his name appears on line three of page thirteen of volume 3942 of the passenger lists. The information given on these post-1910 New York index cards, therefore, is: name, age, sex, line number, page number, volume number. Note that there is no name of any ship and no date of arrival.

You write down this information and put roll number 244 of microfilm T621 back in the drawer. (Be sure you put it in the right place in the right drawer!) Then you walk the few steps to the file drawers containing *Passenger and Crew Lists of Vessels Arriving at New York, N.Y., 1897–1957*, micropublication T715 (8,892 rolls). Roll number 1782 of micropublication T715 is labeled "Volumes 3941-3942." You need volume 3942, so you take it and crank it through to volume 3942, crank to page 13, and then look down the page to line three: there is Domenico Geraci!

SS. Martha Washington. Courtesy of Steamship Historical Society Collection, University of Baltimore.

He appears as a passenger on board the SS. *Martha Washington,* which sailed from Palermo, Sicily, on 21 November 1911, and entered New York on 5 December 1911. His name, age, and year of arrival all fit, but you still want an additional fact to corroborate that this Domenico Geraci is yours. One such "identifying fact" appears in column 11 of the list, which indicates that Domenico's "nearest relative or friend in country whence alien came" is his wife, Rosalia Marrone, and you know from prior research that your ancestor's wife was named Rosalia Marrone.

The volume number derives from the fact that the old ship passenger lists were at one time gathered into volumes, which were then paginated as *volumes.* Do not let the pagination confuse you. Each individual passenger list had its own original page numbers. After being gathered together into a volume, the entire batch of passenger lists was paginated as a volume. Consequently, every page of every passenger list after the first one in the volume has two numbers. It is the volume page number that is of interest to you, regardless of what number that page may happen to be of the individual list.

It is helpful, especially when dealing with common names, to know which volume numbers correspond to which years. Pages 55 through 121 of *Immigrant and Passenger Arrivals* show this correspondence from Volume 1 (beginning 16 June 1897) through Volume 18654 (27 November 1954).

Using the Soundex indexes to ship passenger lists is no more complicated than using the alphabetical indexes, unless your ancestor arrived after 1910 at the port of New York. In that case, interpreting the information printed on the index card takes a little extra effort.

Book Indexes

In addition to the alphabetical and Soundex indexes already discussed, there are also "book indexes" to passenger arrivals at five ports:

Boston: 1899–1940 (1901 is missing)
New York: 1906–1942
Philadelphia: 1906–1926
Portland, Maine: 1907–1930
Providence, Rhode Island: 1911–1934

These indexes, too, were prepared for the Immigration and Naturalization Service, but not by the WPA. They were created by the various steamship lines. They have been microfilmed and are available for searching at the National Archives.

Book indexes are arranged chronologically by year. Under each year, they are grouped by steamship line. Within each line, they are chronological by the date of arrival of each ship. Finally, for each ship, the names of the passengers on board are listed in alphabetical order, albeit by the first letter only of the surname. For each passenger, an age and destination is indicated, but no more than that. For this reason, book indexes are most useful when you know not only your ancestor's approximate date of arrival in the United States, but the most likely steamship line as well. Then, after discovering from the book index the name of your ancestor's ship, and her port and date of arrival, you may examine the original passenger list for all of the additional information it contains.

Problems with the National Archives Indexes—and Solutions

There are many reasons why you may, from time to time, be baffled by the National Archives indexes to ship passenger lists. For example, you may know for sure that your ancestor arrived at a port during a year that is indexed, and not find your ancestor's name in the index.

For one thing, your ancestor's ship passenger list may have been destroyed or lost long before the lists were ever indexed. As noted earlier, an undetermined percentage of all lists created between 1820 and 1957 is lacking from the National Archives' collection. What this means is that if your ancestor arrived, say, at Baltimore in 1827, but his name appeared in a list that was destroyed or lost before the lists were indexed, neither your ancestor's name nor the name of any other passenger traveling on that ship would appear in any index, even though passenger arrivals at the port of Baltimore during 1827 are supposedly indexed. The WPA workers could only include in their indexes, of course, the names that appeared in the lists supplied to them.

In addition, many of the lists in the custody of the Customs Service and the Immigration and Naturalization Service were already in a state of serious deterioration when they were indexed during the Depression. The ink had faded, the pages were brittle or ripped, some having been folded over for decades; corners were torn away, some sheets were missing altogether. A name that happened to be penned where a crease or tear occurred, for example, or a name that had been disfigured by a water stain, may not have been legible to the indexer. So the name, even though it appears in a list that was indexed, does not appear in the index.

Another consideration to keep in mind is that a name may appear differently in the index than it does in the list. The lists were written in a variety of archaic handwritings, some very fine, many very faint, and it was not always possible for the American indexers of the mid-twentieth century to decipher the spelling of every name. They may have mistaken an "o" for an "a," or worse, an initial "G" for a "C," thus entering into the index a surname that does not even exist on any list!

Solutions

If you know that your ancestor arrived at a port that is indexed for his or her year of arrival, but you are unable to find your ancestor's name in that index, you might consider the following techniques.

Try to discover whether your ancestor was traveling with someone—perhaps a relative or neighbor from the native town. Find the name of the traveling companion in the index and note the name of his or her ship and the date of arrival. Then search the passenger list of that ship line by line; chances are you will find your ancestor enumerated right next to the traveling companion—although your ancestor's name may be spelled very creatively!

Try another port. A busy coastal steamer service connected American ports. Passengers arriving at one port sometimes continued on to another port after completing immigration processing. If your grandmother insists that she arrived in Boston, for example, and you do not find her name in the index to Boston arrivals, consider the possibility that she actually entered New York, and then proceeded to Boston by coastal steamer. In that case, her name would be in the index to passenger arrivals at the port of New York, not Boston.

Many portions of the microfilmed indexes at the National Archives are also illegible or almost illegible due to poor microfilming and subsequent use and deterioration. Following are a few suggestions for dealing with hard-to-read index cards.

Try using either a microfilm reader that magnifies the image, or a hand-held magnifying glass. Simply enlarging the faint handwriting sometimes makes it clearer.

If necessary, print the enlarged card from the microfilm—as dark and as large as you can—and "white out" all of the extraneous scratches, marks, ink blotches, etc., to make the essential words stand out more clearly.

You might also try placing a buff-colored sheet of paper on the microfilm reader's reading surface. Projecting the handwriting onto a light-colored sheet of paper rather than the harsh white reading surface helps bring out detail.

If you can make out only three or four letters of the name of the ship, copy those letters as you see them, leaving spaces for the letters you cannot decipher. Then search through listings of passenger ships for a name that fits those letters. (See the "Lists of Ships Arriving at American Ports" section of the bibliography for works that list passenger ships.)

Similarly, if you can read the year of arrival, but not the month and day, it is often possible to obtain the complete date from other sources. Two such sources, *Registers of Vessels Arriving at the Port of New York from Foreign Ports, 1789–1919* (micropubliction M1066) and the *Morton Allan Directory of European Passenger Steamship Arrivals,* are explained in detail later in this book.

Working with the National Archives indexes to ship passenger lists calls for patience and persistence. But it is worth the effort. Even though the indexes are far from complete for every port and every year, and are riddled with errors and idiosyncrasies, they remain the most extensive indexes available for searching for individual names in passenger lists of 1820 to 1954. However, if they turn out not to be helpful in your particular search, do not abandon ship! You are far from defeated! There are many other indexes and resources you may use to achieve success in your quest, as chapter 4 will explain.

Chapter Four

Searching Years Not Included in National Archives Indexes

If you know the exact day, month, and year when your ancestor arrived in the United States, as well as the port of his or her arrival, lucky you! You need no index at all. Go straight to the microfilmed lists for that port, select the roll containing your ancestor's arrival date, and search for your ancestor's name in the lists of ships arriving in that port on that date. Unfortunately, it is rare that genealogists will have such precise information when they undertake the search for an ancestor's ship. Most rely on the indexes for success in their search.

Even when you do have the essential facts—perhaps even the name of the ship—you may still fail to find your ancestor's name on the manifest. Why? Most likely, your "facts" are wrong.

For example, if you are taking the date of arrival, port of arrival, or ship's name from your ancestor's naturalization record, bear in mind that the immigrant may have provided this data from memory some years after his or her arrival in the United States. Years may have passed since the event, and the recollection could be inaccurate. The immigrant may have confused the name of the ship with the name of the port of departure or port of arrival, as many ships were named for major European and American cities. The immigrant may have stated the day and month of arrival correctly—it was, after all, a memorable occasion!—but erred in calculating the year of arrival by his or her age, or some other benchmark. If you check that same day and month one or two years earlier, and one or two years later, you may find the right manifest. (It is also not uncommon for the year of immigration found in population censuses to be off by one or two years.)

When your ancestor's name does not appear where it should, you can also check the pagination of the passenger list. See if any pages are missing. Perhaps some pages were too damaged for microfilming or were already lost when the microfilmers got to the list.

Remember, too, that there is sometimes a discrepancy of a day or two in the arrival date of a steamship, which could be explained by any number of circumstances. For example, the harbormaster may have recorded in the register of arriving vessels that the SS. *Karamania* pulled into port on "July 12"; however, since that was at 11:30 p.m., the steerage passengers did not disembark and go through processing until the following morning, so immigration officials noted "July 13" on the passenger list as the ship's arrival date. It also appears that on rare occasions the microfilmers—for whatever reason—simply filmed a ship's list a day or two out of chronological order. Therefore, if the steamship you are seeking does not appear where it should on the microfilm, check a day or two earlier and a day or two later.

There is no doubt about it—even when you think you have enough information to bypass indexes, you may still find yourself resorting to them. However, as noted, the National Archives indexes, marvelously extensive though they are, do not include all ports and all years. When the port and year of an ancestor's arrival is not included in these micropublications, many genealogists abandon the search. They may even resort to searching through an entire year or two of passenger lists, roll by roll, line by line. This may mean searching through ten, fifteen, or more rolls of microfilm—a tedious, exhausting, and eye-straining task.

Method of LAST Resort

Surely, a list-by-list, line-by-line search should be your method of last resort only, and if you are constrained to search this way, never start with January 1st. Months of heaviest immigration took place, first of all, in the spring—March, April, May—and second, in the fall—September, October, November. Third, immigration during the summer months—June, July, August—was greatly reduced, and last relatively few immigrants came during the cold, foggy, drizzly, snowy, winter—December, January, February—when icebergs littered the North Atlantic. Even searching in this logical order, however—(1) spring, (2) fall, (3) summer, (4) winter—you still may not come upon an ancestor's name until you reach late February. And by that time, you are so blurry-eyed and nodding from fatigue that you may well miss the name altogether!

The mind-numbing job of searching through list after list, line by line, may be made easier if you can eliminate from the start the lists of ships that originated in ports your ancestor would probably not have used when he or she emigrated. Or, better yet, if you know your ancestor's precise port of departure you can ignore all lists except those for ships that originated in that port. (For more about ports of embarkation, see "Emigration Lists" on page 97.)

Nevertheless, even when you know the port of embarkation, searching through many rolls of faded and tattered, handwritten manifests, passenger by passenger, can be prohibitively burdensome. Before you resort to this desperate measure, you should explore the many more efficient—and perhaps ultimately more reliable—strategies for dealing with years not included in National Archives indexes. This chapter discusses those alternative resources and methods. To make the most of them, however, you must analyze your search.

Analyzing Your Search

This is how to analyze your search:

- Evaluate each one of the following resources by asking yourself, "What facts must I know about my ancestor's immigration story to use this resource?"
- Select resources to use based on the facts you know.
- Arrange those resources in descending order, from the most likely to lead to success to the least promising.
- Begin with the first!

Published Arrival Lists and Indexes

Chapter 2 focused on published *pre*-1820 arrival information available in libraries, and the name indexes that have been created to help searchers find specific immigrants within that broad and multifarious literature. In addition to these works, libraries also hold an ever-increasing number of volumes of transcribed or abstracted federal arrival records dating *since* 1820, with a name index in the back of each volume. There are also name index books for other, as yet unpublished, federal arrival records.

These commercially published books—many of which are large multi-volume sets—tend to focus on years that are not covered by National Archives indexes. Each one is limited to passengers of a particular nationality, passengers arriving at a particular port, or passengers arriving during a particular span of years. Although some of these books overlap the microfilmed National Archives indexes (indeed, some are simple transcriptions), most of them complement National Archives indexes by "filling in the gaps." These are the ones that may be decisively helpful to family historians searching for an ancestor in a year for which no National Archives index exists. (See Section II of the bibliography, "Published Arrival Lists and Indexes.")

As long as you know your immigrant ancestor's full original name, approximate age at arrival, and approximate date of arrival, you are prepared to use these published arrival lists and indexes. Perhaps the largest, most general, and most easily accessible of the indexes is P. William Filby's *Passenger and Immigration Lists Index*, which has already been discussed with reference to pre-1820 arrivals (Guillaume Bechet of Louisiana served as a sample research case). Note, however, that well over half of the several million entries in this huge set of volumes pertain to immigrants who arrived *after* 1820. Furthermore, "Filby"—as it is familiarly known—indexes hundreds of published sources that genealogists simply would not find any other way. For these reasons, "Filby" is the first index genealogists turn to when all they have to go on are the three fundamental facts: name, approximate age, and approximate date of arrival.

However, the example searches already explained in this manual demonstrate that the more you know about the immigration story, the more you can narrow your search. Following are two research scenarios that demonstrate how to use published lists and indexes to find your ancestor in a National Archives ship passenger list when you know some additional fact, such as your ancestor's nationality or port of arrival. For each work suggested, refer to the bibliography for complete publication data and annotations. As always when using any reference text, be sure to read the introduction carefully to understand precisely what records are included and precisely how they are indexed.

For instance, *Germans to America* does not by any means name all Germans who came to the United States during the years covered by the series. For the period 1850 through 1855, the books reproduce the entire passenger lists of ships carrying a minimum of eighty percent "German" surnames. Persons with "German" surnames may be natives of Belgium, France, Luxembourg, Switzerland, or any one of the numerous German states and principalities. The lists reproduced in these early volumes, therefore, include up to twenty percent non-German names. By the time the project reached the lists of 1856, however, the series' editors decided to change the criteria of their project. Rather than limit their indexing to lists of ships with a minimum of eighty percent "German" surnames, they would index all ships carrying any number of German-surnamed passengers. They would transcribe—not the entire lists—but only the "German" surnames from those lists. For the period since 1856, therefore, no non-German names appear in *Germans to America*. Be sure to always read the introduction, because book titles alone may be misleading!

If You Know Your Ancestor's Nationality

Search for your ancestor's name in abstracts and indexes compiled by nationality, such as:

Glazier, Ira A., ed. *The Famine Immigrants: Lists of Irish Immigrants Arriving at the Port of New York, 1846–1851.* 7 vols.

Glazier, Ira A., and P. William Filby, eds. *Germans to America: Lists of Passengers Arriving at U.S. Ports.* Published to date—1850–1892. 63 vols.

Avakian, Linda L. *Armenian Immigrants, Boston 1891–1901*, New York 1880-1897.

If You Know Your Ancestor's Port of Arrival

Search for your ancestor's name in abstracts and indexes compiled by port of arrival, such as:

Rasmussen, Louis J. *San Francisco Ship Passenger Lists.* Published to date—1850–1875.

Galveston County Genealogical Society. *Ship Passenger Lists, Port of Galveston, Texas, 1846–1871.*

Holcomb, Brent H. *Passenger Arrivals at the Port of Charleston, 1820–1829.*

Note that each of these works focuses on a specific national group, port, and span of years. They are far from comprehensive. Nevertheless, the time periods they cover complement the years covered by National Archives indexes, which may make such a work the critical element to success in your quest. Some are ongoing, with a new volume appearing every year. So if your ancestor's year has not yet been covered, you may only have to be patient and wait for the next volume!

If you find your ancestor's name in one of these works of transcribed and indexed lists, step one of your search is done. Proceed to step two: use the data provided to locate the National Archives passenger list. Place the pertinent roll of microfilm in the reader and find your ancestor's name in the list; then, double-check the information you find there against your ancestor's full original name, approximate age at arrival, approximate date of arrival, and any additional information you know about the immigration story to be certain the passenger is your ancestor and not someone else's!

Useful as these commercially published, multi-volume works are to family historians, it is wise to bear in mind—especially when you do not find your ancestor's name in them—that they contain many errors. The people transcribing the names are not always adept at reading the faint, archaic, often European scripts, or—in the case of *Germans to America*—at recognizing which surnames may reasonably be considered "German." There appears to be only the most cursory of editorial control or oversight for these ambitious, ongoing publications. For example, the original passenger list on microfilm of the ship

South America, which arrived in New York on 21 May 1853, shows one "Geo. Ring" on board. The list as it appears in *Germans to America* (vol. 4, p. 463) reveals that fully twenty percent of the surnames had been incorrectly transcribed. "Geo. Ring" appears in the index as "RINZ, GEORG." Other volumes of the set, however, may have a much higher rate of accuracy.

How do you search for an ancestor's ship when there is no National Archives index and no published lists or index covering the port and years of interest to you? There are many more resources at your disposal!

CD-ROM Indexes

Modern technology has changed, and continues to change, the way genealogists access the information they need to find passenger arrival records. Today, an efficient and productive search for an ancestor's ship entails using the latest electronic tools available—CD-ROMs and the Internet—in conjunction with the traditional materials already discussed—paper and microform. Tried-and-true principles of sound methodology still apply! Whether using old materials or new, always bring to your search a healthy dose of skepticism: look to see where the editor, compiler, home pager, or publisher found the information, and then make every effort to examine that original source yourself. This section explores useful materials in CD-ROM format; the following section will deal with the Internet.

Many of the CD-ROM indexes to passenger arrival records are simply publications in electronic format of works already available in print or microform. While they provide nothing new, they do offer greater convenience, because each CD-ROM has a "search engine" that makes looking up a specific name very easy. What's more, you may view CD-ROMs on your home computer at your pleasure and print out any entries you wish to pursue.

Here are five examples:

- Filby's *Passenger and Immigration Lists Index*, the huge, multi-volume set containing over 3,000,000 names of immigrants appearing in published literature is now available as CD #354 by Genealogy.com (formerly Brøderbund publishing as *Family Tree Maker*). Rather than pore through the books, you may purchase the entire set on this single CD.

- Coldham's *Complete Book of Emigrants* (4 vols.) and *Complete Book of Emigrants in Bondage* (1 vol. and supplement) have been published jointly by Genealogical Publishing Company and Genealogy.com as CD #350. It is titled *The Complete Book of Emigrants, 1607–1776*, and it contains approximately 140,000 names of men, women and children who emigrated from England to America during colonial times.

- Five of Genealogical Publishing Company's books—*New World Immigrants*, vols. 1 and 2; *Emigrants to Pennsylvania, 1641–1819*; *Immigrants to the Middle Colonies*; and *Passengers to America*—have been published jointly by Genealogical Publishing Company and Genealogy.com as CD #170. It is titled *Immigrants to the New World, 1600s–1800s*.

- Glazier and Filby's ongoing set, *Germans to America*, is available as CDs #355 (1850–74) and #356 (1875–88).

- Michael Tepper's *Passenger Arrivals at the Port of Baltimore, 1820-1834*, has been reissued and expanded to include sixteen additional years on CD #259, *Passenger and Immigration Lists, Baltimore, 1820–1852* (about 89,000 names).

Other CD-ROM indexes, however, are entirely new publications covering years not included in any book or National Archives index. Here are two examples:

- *Passenger and Immigration Lists: Boston, 1821–1850* (#256, about 161,000 names)

- *Passenger and Immigration Lists: New Orleans, 1820–1850* (#358, about 258,000 names).

These CDs are alphabetical name indexes to passengers who arrived during the years specified in the titles. For each name, essential identifying information is given, as well as the National Archives micropublication number and roll where that passenger may be found on the list. These CDs were compiled from the microfilmed lists themselves (rather than pre-existing indexes or other derivative materials). This makes them a major contribution to the field because, as chapter 3 pointed out, not all pre-1848 Boston arrivals, and not all pre-1853 New Orleans arrivals, are included in National Archives indexes. Some are indexed in the *Supplemental Index to … Atlantic and Gulf Coast Ports, 1820–1874* (M233), but not all. A two-volume set by Milton P. and Norma G. Reider, *New Orleans Ship Lists*, covered arrivals of January 1820 through June 1823 only. Now these two CDs fill in the rest of the wide gaps in Boston and New Orleans indexes! Sometimes, however, CDs do not provide as much information as the older media. For instance, the data for Thomas Morley, a twenty-two-year-old Irishman arriving in Boston in 1846, given in *Passenger and Immigration Lists: Boston, 1821–1850*, is this: name, country of origin, gender, arrival date, age, and occupation, followed by "Microfilm source, Series M277, Roll 20." What is not given, however, is the name of his ship! So you have to search through the lists of all ships arriving on 5 May 1846, until you come to Thomas Morley on one of them. Had you used National Archives index M233, the *Supplemental Index*, you would have found a card for Thomas Morley that provided the name of his ship, the *Governor Davis*, thus reducing your search to only one list rather than a whole day's worth of lists. Note, however, that the CDs for Baltimore and New Orleans do provide the name of the ship.

Works available in CD-ROM format are highlighted as such in the bibliography; there are many more of them than the few examples already cited. However, since new electronic materials are appearing all the time, you may wish to visit the websites of the major CD-ROM publishers for the latest update. Which brings us to the Internet.

American Family Immigration History Center and Other Websites

What is perhaps the most far-reaching advance in immigrant ancestor research since the WPA indexing projects of the 1930s debuted on the Internet in the spring of 2001: <www.ellisislandrecords.org>. This is the website of the American Family Immigration History Center at Ellis Island, prepared by thousands of volunteers of The Church of Jesus Christ of Latter-day Saints working for more than a decade under the aegis of the Statue of Liberty—Ellis Island Foundation, Inc. It contains digitized images of the passenger arrival records of New York for the years when Ellis Island served as the immigrant receiving station, 1892–1924. (For a brief history of Ellis Island, see the Conclusion, "Ellis Island: What's Myth? What's Reality?") These New York manifests contain an estimated twenty-two million names. Besides the digitized lists, however, the website contains a transcription of nine facts for every passenger named on them, as well as a search engine for "zeroing in" on one passenger among the millions. In short, it works as follows:

Patrick Sheehan was 48 when he crossed the Atlantic on the steamship Aurania. The passenger list for his voyage bears the date 21 February 1893; however, the New York Times reveals that the ship actually pulled into the harbor on the afternoon of the 20th. It appears that the ship was not "recorded" and the steerage passengers did not go through processing until the 21st. This was often the case when many ships pulled in at about the same time; they had to be taken one at a time, so some had to wait.

On the site's initial screen, under "Find a Passenger," key in the name of the ancestor you seek. In a few seconds a roster of all passengers by that name found in the database will be displayed with each one's residence, year of arrival, and age at arrival. Using that information, select the passenger you believe is your ancestor, and click on that name. A screen will appear showing the nine transcribed items of information for that passenger. If the data "fit" your ancestor, click on "Ship Manifest," and the digitized passenger list appears for you to enlarge and examine.

The tremendous power of this finding aide boggles the mind! Ellisislandrecords.org simplifies to an astounding degree the search for New York arrivals during a span of years (1892–1924) that includes years for which no comprehensive index existed (1892–1896), and years for which the microfilmed index that does exist is so unclear as to be virtually useless in most cases (1897–1902). Certainly, as with all research tools, electronic or print, shortcomings do exist. A commendable effort was made to double-check the transcription of all information before entering it into the database, and to devise a search engine that would help the user find a passenger even when the spelling of the surname is uncertain or may vary. The user may instruct the search engine to bring up all surnames that begin with a certain letter combination, for example, or that end in a certain letter combination, or that are close in spelling, and so forth. Be aware, however, that success in every search cannot be guaranteed.

Numerous names, particularly the names of eastern European passengers, were transcribed incorrectly, and the website's search engine does not offer as broad a scanning capability as would be desirable for finding passengers whose names, for one reason of another, do not appear as the researcher expects them to. To remedy these problems, parties not associated with the American Family Immigration History Center have devised search engines that, working in conjunction with the website's engine, enhance the possibility of locating hard-to-find ancestors. For in-depth analysis and search strategies, see the *FORUM* article by Gary Mokotoff cited in the bibliography, as well as the discussions appearing on the website of the Federation of Eastern European Family History Societies <www.feefhs.org> and the website for Jewish Genealogy <www.jewishgen.com>.

Nor is Ellisislandrecords.org by any means the only website helpful to Americans seeking the ships of their immigrant forebears! While New York City saw the lion's share of immigration, it was only one port among many, and 1892–1924, though peak years of immigration, was only one era in a much longer history. As discussed in chapter 2 earlier, Cyndi's List of Genealogy Sites on the Internet <www.cyndislist.com/ships.htm> is a good place to begin searching for websites that may prove helpful in finding an ancestor's ship. It links to numerous sites with information about ships, passenger lists, and crew lists. Following is just a sampling of helpful websites. Others will be cited later in this chapter. And, surely, new ones are appearing all the time!

The website of the National Archives <www.nara.gov> contains the entire *Guide to Federal Records in the National Archives of the United States,* all of the catalogs of microfilm (including *Immigrant & Passenger Arrivals*), and excellent essays, not only on passenger arrival records, but on a variety of other records of value for finding an ancestor's ship, such as naturalization records, homestead records, and passport applications. It is a simple matter, for example, to check online to see

whether the CD-ROM index, *Passenger and Immigration Lists: Boston, 1821-1850*, is correct in indicating that Thomas Morley's ship, arriving on 5 May 1846, is found on National Archives micropublication M277, roll 20. The online catalog, *Immigrant & Passenger Arrivals*, confirms this information.

The personal website of Illya James D'Addezio <www.daddezio. co> links to several hundred ship passenger lists posted on the Internet. However, beware of third- and fourth-hand materials! Always look for the source of information, and then access the original record to confirm accuracy. Be warned that D'Addezio's alphabetical "Directory of Passenger Ship Arrivals" is imprecise. It includes "pink" and "snow" as part of a ship's name—the *Pink Rose*, the *Snow George*— when these are types of sailing vessels. The ship is not the *Pink Rose*, but the *Rose*, which happens to be a pink (a type of ship). The ship is not the *Snow George*, but the *George*, which happens to be a snow (another type of ship). The error is repeated many times.

But we can use this site to learn whether the list of Thomas Morley's ship, the *Governor Davis*, is transcribed somewhere on the Internet. It is! D'Addezio links us directly with the "Immigrant Ships Transcribers Guild" page containing the list of the "Gov. Davis"! (The "Immigrant Ships Transcribers Guild" <www.istg.rootsweb.com> is discussed in chapter 2.) But is this the list for Thomas Morley's Liverpool-to-Boston crossing of April–May 1846, or some other crossing? It turns out to be the list of a Liverpool-to-Boston crossing, sure enough, but one made in 1847—a year too late to be the list with Thomas Morley's name on it! You see how passenger arrival information research on the Internet is "catch-as-catch-can."

Hamburg Emigration Lists (1850-1934) are discussed in detail below under the heading, "Emigration Lists." However, since they are now being transcribed and up-loaded to the Internet, they must be mentioned here as well. The website is <www.hamburg.de/

LinkToYourRoots/english/welcome.htm> and as of the printing of this book, the lists of 1890 through 1893 have been completed. Let us say you are looking for your Bavarian ancestor named Christoph Mueller, who you know came to the United States around 1891 with his wife and children. Simply click on "Search for Passenger," fill in the blanks with the information requested, such as family name, given name, gender, approximate year of birth, etc., and then click on "Run Report." If a passenger of that description appears on the Hamburg Emigration Lists, a screen will appear displaying the information about him contained on the list: place of residence (town), state of residence (German state or foreign country), profession, place of destination, date of departure, ship's destination, ship's name, shipping company, accommodation (cabin class or steerage), and more. And there he is—your Christoph Mueller! He is listed under the original spelling of his surname, Müller, with his wife and children in steerage

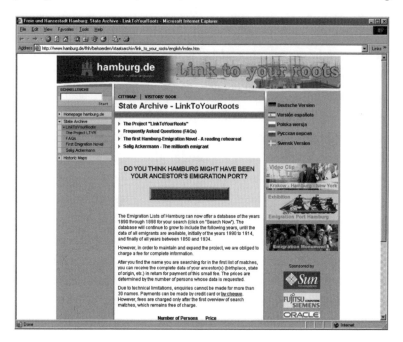

aboard the steamship *Augusta Victoria*. The *Augusta Victoria* left Hamburg for New York on "04.09.91"—that is, on 4 September 1891 (note that the date is given in the European fashion—day/month/year—as these are German records). To find the passenger arrival list in the National Archives microfilm, you need to learn when the *Augusta Victoria* arrived in New York. Here's where another website comes in handy...

The *Morton Allan Directory of Passenger Steamship Arrivals* is also discussed later, but is referred to here in brief because it, too, is available on the Internet. The website is <www.cimorelli.com/safe/shipmenu.htm>, the personal website of Anthony J. Cimorelli. Searching for the steamship *Augusta Victoria* in the year 1891 results in six arrival dates. Since you already know the steamship left Hamburg on 4 September, the arrival date that fits is "9/14/1891" (note that the date is given in the American way—month/day/year—as the *Morton Allan Directory* is a U.S. publication). Now all you have to do is consult the New York lists (National Archives micropublication M237, roll 575) to see Christoph Mueller's arrival record, or you can also write to the National Archives (using NATF Form 81) for a print of the page containing his name. Your final step would be to obtain a picture of the *Augusta Victoria*. While some Internet websites provide images of ships, these will be discussed in chapter 5, under the heading, "Obtaining a Picture of Your Ancestor's Ship."

The outstanding website of The Church of Jesus Christ of Latter-day Saints <www.familysearch.org> provides the LDS Family History Library's entire catalog, plus enormous databases of millions of names, plus research tools—such as manuals for researching in the records of the fifty states and foreign countries, genealogical word lists and sample letters in foreign languages, plus a good deal of extremely useful instruction. At your leisure, in the comfort of your own home, you may search to see what passenger arrival information the library has on microfilm, and then proceed to borrow it at any Family History Center worldwide. As already stated in the Introduction, the LDS Family History Library collection includes copies of all of the micropublications discussed in this manual.

Indianola Immigrant Database <www.indianolabulletin.com/immigrantdatabase.htm> contains about 1,500 names of immigrants who, according to oral family lore or some written source, arrived at Indianola, Texas, before that port and all of its official records were destroyed by a hurricane in 1886. The project is ongoing.

Finally, the website of Earnie Lang, which is at <http://home.att.net/%7Earnielang/shipgide.html> contains excellent instruction on how to find an immigrant ancestor's arrival record.

This sampling of useful websites is selective; many others may prove helpful in your search. Remember, every immigrant ancestor was an individual with his or her own story, so every search for an ancestor's ship is unique. In addition, other resources have long been extremely helpful in finding the ship of a forebear who arrived in a year that is not included in any National Archives index. An examination of these resources follows.

Registers of Vessels Arriving at the Port of New York

If your ancestor arrived at the port of New York in a year for which there is no National Archives index—1847 through 1896, inclusive—one useful tool is micropublication M1066, *Registers of Vessels Arriving at the Port of New York from Foreign Ports, 1789–1919* (twenty-seven rolls). This is the most complete list available of the ships that entered New York from foreign ports between 1789 and 1919. A portion of it appears in book form under the title *Passenger Ships Arriving in New York Harbor (1820–1850)*, edited by Bradley W. Steuart. This same portion, plus a smattering of other years, also appears on the Internet <www.cimorelli.com/safe/shipmenu.htm> (referred to earlier).

Any publication comprised of so many volumes of records, created by a variety of offices for a variety of purposes over a time period exceeding a century, will inevitably contain many inconsistencies. These volumes vary a great deal in their internal arrangement, as well as in the amount and type of information they record. Most of the volumes contain at least the following for each vessel listed: name, country of origin, type of rig, date of entry, master's name, and initial port of embarkation. Some volumes, however, contain additional information as well. For most years the ships are listed in strict chronological order of arrival; for a few years the ships may be listed in alphabetical order, regardless of their exact date of arrival, or they may be grouped by steamship line.

Regardless of how the information is arranged, *Registers of Vessels Arriving at the Port of New York* may be helpful in your search if you know: (1) the name of your ancestor's ship; or (2) the ship's exact date of arrival; or (3) your ancestor's port of departure. To demonstrate, let us say your ancestor Andreas Schlager came from Bavaria in 1886 with his wife, Ursula. You have searched the National Archives indexes, as well as published book indexes, CD-ROMs and the Internet, all without success. Now you turn to M1066.

If You Know the Name of the Ship

Select the roll of M1066 that corresponds to the year of your ancestor's arrival, and make note of every day on which his or her ship entered New York Harbor that year. Then turn to the New York passenger lists, micropublication M237, and search the lists of your ancestor's ship, one by one, line by line, for the arrival dates you noted. Your ancestor's name should appear in one of them.

In our sample case of Andreas Schlager, you know from oral family tradition that he came on the SS. *Werra*. Using M1066, you learn

Page from a Register of Vessels. *This sample is from National Archives microfilm M1066, Registers of Vessels Arriving at the Port of New York from Foreign Ports, 1789-1919, roll 8, "Jan. 2-Dec. 31, 1856." It shows that the bark Elbe, Captain Winzen, arrived 21 May 1856, from Hamburg, Germany.*

that the SS. *Werra* entered New York Harbor eight times in 1886:

6 March

5 April

1 May

28 May

8 July

23 August

7 October

17 November

Taking the New York passenger lists, micropublication M237, you search the lists of the SS. *Werra* for those eight arrival dates. You find an Andreas Schlager in the list for the crossing that terminated on 28 May 1886. Enumerated with him is his wife, Ursula—proof that you have found your Andreas Schlager, and not someone else's.

When dealing with sailing vessels in earlier years, you will probably not collect more than three to five dates, since rigged vessels made fewer crossings each year than the later, faster steamships. (See "Sailing Vessels and Steamships" on page 94.)

This same strategy may be used in reverse: when you do not know the name of the ship, but you do know the exact date of arrival.

If You Know the Exact Date of Arrival

You know from Andreas Schlager's petition for naturalization that he arrived at the port of New York on 28 May 1886, but you do not know in what ship. Select the roll of M1066 that contains the date 28 May 1886 and make note of every ship that entered New York Harbor that day. It turns out to be twelve ships in all.

Eliminate all the unlikely candidates: three ships arrived from South American ports (Rio de Janeiro, Brazil; Cartagena, Colombia;

Montevideo, Uruguay); three ships came from the Caribbean (Havanna and Cienfuegos, Cuba; Kingston, Jamaica); two from the Orient (Yokohama, Japan; Hong Kong); one from Marseilles, France; one from Liverpool, England. Eliminating those unlikely ships leaves two possibilities: the SS. *Moravia* out of Hamburg, and the SS. *Werra* out of Bremen.

Turn then to the New York passenger lists, micropublication M237, and search the lists of those two liners. You discover Andreas and Ursula Schlager on board the SS. *Werra*.

Even if you do not know the name of your forebear's ship or the exact date of arrival, *Registers of Vessels Arriving at the Port of New York* may still be useful if you know from which port your ancestor emigrated.

If You Know the Port of Embarkation

Since Andreas Schlager was Bavarian by birth, it is most likely that he emigrated from the port of Bremen. (For tips on determining an ancestor's probable port of departure, see "Emigration Lists" later in this chapter.) Using micropublication M1066, select from all of the passenger ships arriving in New York in 1886 only those that originated in Bremen. Search the lists of these ships for your forefather, and you will find him on the SS. *Werra*.

Be advised, however, that this strategy may still leave you with an unmanageable number of lists to search if your ancestor left from a *busy* port in the *late* nineteenth century—as did Andreas Schlager. By 1886, ships from Bremen were entering New York Harbor about ninety-five times a year. It is possible, of course, that your ancestor came on one of the early voyages, so you will not have to search through all ninety-five lists. On the other hand, he may have come right around the middle of the year—28 May—as did Andreas Schlager. But then, he may have come on the very last crossing of the year, too. ...

For this reason, one valuable tool may be the *Registers of Vessels Arriving at the Port of New York* because searching through two or three, even fifteen or twenty—and perhaps as many as ninety-five!—passenger lists is far preferable to searching through thirteen or fourteen entire rolls of microfilm. The fact that portions of M1066 are now available in print and online makes this search tool easier than ever to access.

Lists of Vessels Arriving at Ports Other Than New York

The National Archives also has journals of, and alphabetical indexes to, vessels arriving at ports other than New York. These include Boston, Philadelphia, Baltimore, and New Orleans, and are part of Record Group 36, Records of the U.S. Customs Service. None have been organized and microfilmed as New York's have, but portions of them have appeared in print form. For instance, listings of ships arriving at Baltimore, 1820-1891, and Boston, 1820-1860, are printed in the work compiled by Lawrence B. Bangerter cited in the bibliography.

Sailing Vessels and Steamships

As the example of Andreas Schlager shows, it may prove helpful to your search to know whether your ancestor arrived in a sailing vessel or a steamship. Steamships began making regular crossings of the Atlantic in the 1850s. Steamship companies advertised that they could maintain a regular schedule, regardless of wind and current, and steamships crossed the ocean in less than half the time it took sailing vessels. But the transatlantic fares of sailing ships remained for many years much cheaper than those of steamships, so many immigrants, most of whom were poor, continued into the 1870s to endure the discomfort and uncertainty of reaching the United States under sail. By the 1880s, however, steam had effectively replaced sail forever.

Depending on her tonnage, how much sail she carried, and the winds and ocean currents, a sailing vessel might take anywhere from four to twelve weeks to cross the Atlantic. Persistent adverse winds and major storms could drag the crossing out even longer. A normal, uneventful transatlantic voyage by sail lasted seven to eight weeks. Steamships crossed in two to three weeks during the nineteenth century, depending on the number of intermediate ports the vessel visited on her way to the United States. That travel time was shortened to one week by the time of World War I, and by the 1920s steamships from Europe could reach America in just five days.

The Morton Allan Directory

Another resource for finding an ancestor's ship when the indexes prove unhelpful is the *Morton Allan Directory of European Passenger Steamship Arrivals*. This volume is similar to M1066 and the registers of vessels arriving at other ports (yet unmicrofilmed), and may be used in a similar fashion. It lists by year, and thereunder by steamship line, the names and dates of arrival of all vessels that came from Europe to New York from 1890 to 1930, and to Baltimore, Boston, and Philadelphia from 1904 to 1926. If you know that your ancestor arrived at one of these ports in one of these years, you may implement any one of the following three strategies:

If You Know the Name of the Ship

Note every date when that ship arrived during the year when your ancestor came to America, then search through those lists.

If You Know the Exact Date of Arrival

Note the names of all ships that arrived on that date, eliminate the unlikely ones, then search through the lists of the remaining ships.

If You Know the Port of Embarkation

Under each steamship line, all vessels arriving from the same European port or ports are given in the same chronological list. In 1920, for example, all Holland-America Line ships ran between Rotterdam and New York, so they are all given in one chronological list. On twenty-six different dates between 23 January and 20 December 1920, a Holland-America steamship pulled into New York Harbor. The Cunard Line, by contrast, was far larger. On seventy-five occasions during 1920 a Cunard ship pulled into a U.S. port. But these seventy-five arrivals are given in five different chronological lists, because the steamships traveled five different itineraries: Liverpool to New York; Southampton to New York; Cherbourg-Plymouth-London-Hamburg to New York; Mediterranean ports to New York; and London to Boston.

Given this format, therefore, the *Morton Allan Directory* may be used as follows: (1) turn to the year when your ancestor came to the United States; (2) from all of the ships arriving that year, select only those originating in your ancestor's most likely port of debarkation; (3) then search the lists of those ships. (As noted in the Andreas Schlager example using National Archives micropublication M1066, this strategy may still not reduce the number of lists to a number practical for searching if your ancestor left from a very busy European port.)

The *Morton Allan Directory*—along with other vessel arrival records—may prove useful in other ways as well, depending on your research scenario and how creative a researcher you are. For example, you may use it to verify or correct arrival information.

I was once searching for an immigrant who arrived in 1928, according to the story she told her children. She remembered the name of the ship she sailed on, and maintained that she entered the United States at the port of New York. But my research showed that no ship by that name arrived in New York at that time. Finding the ship in the *Morton Allan Directory*, I discovered that she regularly entered the port of

Boston—not New York—and I noted the precise dates in 1928 when she arrived. Then I turned to the microfilmed passenger lists for Boston (micropublication T843), searched the lists for those arrival dates, and found the name of the immigrant I sought. Given this information, it seems likely that the woman, upon disembarking in Boston, immediately boarded a coastal steamer for New York, where family was expecting her, and that is why she considered New York her port of entry.

Furthermore, note that some steamships arrived at two ports just a day or two apart, discharging some passengers at each port.

Galveston Immigrant Database

The Texas Seaport Museum, 2016 Strand, Galveston, TX 77550, has an "Immigrant Database" that contains 130,000 names of people who arrived at the port of Galveston between 1846 and 1948. It may be used at the museum, but is not available at the museum's website <www.tsm-elissa.org>. The database was compiled from a breadth of sources, including National Archives micropublications, published book indexes (See Leo Baca and Albert Blaha, for example, in the bibliography at the end of this manual), histories and other scholarly studies, journal articles, and even unpublished theses and dissertations, making it a more complete index to passenger arrivals at the port of Galveston than are the National Archives indexes alone.

Although a variety of foreign nationals entered Galveston, of particular interest to American Jews seeking the ships of their ancestors is the "Galveston Project," a humanitarian venture that ushered about 10,000 Jews from their homes in Eastern Europe through the port of Bremen and into Galveston between 1907 and 1918.

Emigration Lists

"Ship passenger lists," "passenger arrival lists," "passenger arrival records," "immigration lists"—these are all terms used to denote (with varying degrees of accuracy) the enormous body of microfilmed Customs Passenger Lists and Immigration Passenger Lists in the National Archives, because these records enumerate people arriving in the United States from foreign ports. However, ports of embarkation overseas also kept records, records of passengers departing for foreign destinations, including the United States. Such "emigration lists" constitute another valuable tool for finding an ancestor's ship when National Archives indexes, book indexes, CD-ROMs, and the Internet prove unhelpful.

Determining Your Ancestor's Probable Port of Departure

To determine through which port your ancestor may have emigrated to North America, you must know where he or she resided prior to departure. A reputable history of your ancestor's homeland will explain when emigration movements occurred, and what route the emigrants followed.

For instance, during the 1700s and into the 1820s, German-speaking emigrants from central Europe—Switzerland, Wuerttemberg, Baden, Alsace, Lorraine, Luxembourg, the Palatinate, and Rhineland—generally took a boat down the Rhine River to Rotterdam or Antwerp and sailed to North America from there. Traveling by water was the cheapest (albeit the slowest) way to get to a port city. By the 1840s, however, railroads in France and Germany had made traveling overland from the city of Strasbourg on the Rhine to the northern French port of Le Havre on the English Channel more attractive than the earlier river route. A faster journey meant less money expended on food and lodging. From that time, Le Havre replaced Rotterdam and Antwerp as the most probable port of departure for emigrants from the Central European region along the Rhine.

Or, for another example, during the 1860s and 1870s, before transatlantic liners sailed from Scandinavian ports directly to the

United States, Norwegian and Swedish emigrants usually crossed the North Sea on a local steamer to Scotland or England, traversed the country by train, then sailed out of Glasgow or Liverpool on a steamship to America. An alternate route, particularly convenient for Danes, was to take a local steamer to the northern German port of Bremen or Hamburg, and there board a ship bound for the United States.

Karl Wittke's *We Who Built America: The Saga of the American Immigrant* (See bibliography) discusses the emigration routes of a variety of national groups from Europe. A history devoted solely to your own ancestor's national group, however, is more likely to provide the detailed information you seek.

These same types of works, and the ever-flourishing ethnic histories referred to in chapter 1, frequently provide information about which ports emigrants used to enter North America. Knowing your ancestor's probable port of entry may also prove useful to your search, as noted in the Domenico Geraci example cited in chapter 3.

Locating Emigration Lists

Once you know your ancestor's most probable port of departure, how do you learn whether any emigration lists exist for that port? Begin by looking at chapter 13 of *The Source: A Guidebook of American Genealogy*, 2nd ed. (See bibliography). It includes a table titled "Availability of European Emigrant Lists" (pp. 492–495) which shows the departure records that still exist for many ports of Europe, Australia, and the West Indies, whether they are published, whether they are indexed, and how to access them. For ports not covered in this table, examine a guide to genealogical research for the country whose port interests you.

Bremen Passenger Lists

From the mid-nineteenth century through the early twentieth century, the busiest European port of embarkation was Bremen, Germany.

Millions of emigrants from Northern, Central, and Eastern Europe left from Bremen, and beginning in 1832 the port maintained lists of departing passengers. Unfortunately, the lists created prior to 1910 were routinely destroyed every few years (after statistical data were extracted from them); and the lists created between 1910 (when the German government began preserving them) and 1920 were destroyed in Allied bombing raids during World War II. However, the departure manifests created from 1920 through 1939 have survived. They are preserved at the Handelskammer Archiv in Bremen, and transcriptions of these records are now being posted to the Internet at <http://db.genealogy.net/maus/gate/shiplists.cgi>. So far, 1920 through 1922 are complete, comprising 188 passenger lists, and 1923 through 1925 are in progress. The lists are searchable by passenger name, ship name, departure date, and port of destination. The site is ultimately projected to include all extant lists through 1939.

Regarding pre-1920 Bremen departures, three resources that "reconstruct" portions of the lost Bremen Passenger Lists could be of value to Americans searching for their ancestors' ships.

First, the Deutsches Ausland-Institut in Stuttgart created a card file titled *Namenskartei aus den "Bremer Schiffslisten," 1904-1914*, which today is in the German State Archives in Koblenz. The LDS Family History Library has a copy of this card file on ten reels of microfilm. The cards contain the names of emigrants based on the Bremen Passenger Lists. The first two reels contain cards arranged alphabetically by state—Anhalt-Posen through Wurttemburg—then by surname (not necessarily in alphabetical order). The other eight reels contain cards arranged by country—Austria, Bohemia, Moravia, Hungary, Russia, Jewish Emigrants, and "Other Lands"—then by surname (not necessarily in alphabetical order).

However, note that these cards do not constitute a comprehensive list of emigrants leaving from Bremen. The first two reels name only

German emigrants. The other eight reels covering other nationalities contain only sporatic dates of departure. Nevertheless, this card file contains thousands of emigrants' names and should not be overlooked.

Second, transcripts of a few Bremen Passenger Lists are housed in the German State Archives in Koblenz. They cover March 1907 through November 1908, and portions of the years 1913 and 1914.

Third, Gary Zimmerman and Marion Wolfert have published what might be called a "partial reconstruction" of the Bremen Passenger Lists (See bibliography). Using ship passenger lists at the National Archives, they have extracted the names of German passengers aboard vessels that sailed from Bremen to New York, and listed those names in alphabetical order in four volumes. The volumes cover the years 1847 through 1871. Note, however, that only German passengers for whom a specific place of origin was given in the lists are included in Zimmerman and Wolfert's index—about twenty-one percent of the total number of German passengers leaving the port of Bremen.

Hamburg Passenger Lists

The second busiest port of embarkation from Europe was Hamburg. Happily, the original passenger lists for the port of Hamburg covering the years 1850 through 1934 are still preserved in the State Archives in Hamburg, and they are indexed. These emigration records—probably the most informative and extensive of any European port—are particularly useful to Americans searching for ancestors' ships, since millions of Americans are descended from northern, central and Eastern Europeans who left their homelands between 1850 and 1934 via Hamburg. In addition, as already noted, they are now being uploaded to the Internet (See "American Family Immigration History Center and Other Websites" earlier in this chapter).

The original lists and the indexes to them are gathered into 517 bound volumes. A microfilm copy of these volumes is retained in the

Direct List Index. *This sample page is from LDS Family History Library microfilm 473,000, Index [Direct, Vol. 8], 1855-1856. It shows that Heim Schwien, listed under "12/4 Elbe, Winzen n/New York," can be found (with his wife and children) on page 79 of the direct list.*

Verzeichniss

r Personen, welche mit dem *Hamburger* Schiffe *Elbe*
pitain *Winzen* nach *New York*
zur Auswanderung durch Unterzeichneten engagirt sind.

Zu- und Vorname und Familie.	Geburts- und Wohnort.	Landes.	Gewerbe.	Alter	Ge-schlecht		Total	Recapitula	
					männl.	weibl.		Erwachsene und Kinder über 8 Jahr.	unter 8 Jahr.
Brandeline J.W.	Schweinfurt Bayern			23	1		1	1	
Henning Joh.			Landm	54	1		1	1	
d. Marie			Ehefrau	52		1	1	1	
d. Caroline				15		1	1	1	
d. Fried.	Sarmen	Preußen	Kinder	17	1		1	1	
d. Carl				5	1		1		1
Stephan Carl			Landm	25	1		1	1	
d. Friedr.			ledig	23		1	1	1	
Tufall Doris	Brake	Oldenburg		30		1	1	1	
Linemand Carl	Bückeberg	Hannover	Töpfler	31	1		1	1	
Axel Michael			Landm	25	1		1	1	
d. Wilhelm	Brandelen		Ehefrau	22		1	1	1	
Engel Gottfr.		Preußen	Landm	26	1		1	1	
Frau Charlotte		d.	ledig	22		1	1	1	
Weiß Benj.	Stargard	d.	Müller	24	1		1	1	
Boge Christine	Neustelle	Mecklenburg	ledig	24		1	1	1	
Schwien Heim			Ziegler	54	1		1	1	
d. Marie			Ehefrau	53		1	1	1	
d. August				18	1		1	1	
d. Carl	Herings			13	1		1	1	
d. Caroline	dorf	Holstein	Kinder	11		1	1	1	
d. Johann				2		1	1		1
Husberg Cath			Farin	27		1	1	1	
Opse E.H.	Beschendf		Landm	32	1		1	1	
Schumacher H.	Heringsdorf	d.		21	1		1	1	

Direct List for 1856, Page 79. This is from the LDS Family History Library microfilm 470,838, Passenger Lists [Direct, Vol. 10, Part I], 1856. It shows Heim Schwien and family on lines 17-22.

Historic Emigration Office at the Museum for Hamburg History. (The Historic Emigration Office is established in what used to be the officers' mess of the SS. *Werner*.) A copy of this microfilm is available through the LDS Family History Library. The Library of Congress in Washington, D.C., has a copy of the microfilm for the years 1850 through 1873 only.

The Hamburg lists contain not only the name of each departing passenger's ship, the date of departure and port of destination, but also each passenger's age, birthplace or last residence, and occupation. Therefore, if you find your ancestor in the Hamburg lists, all you need to do to find the ship passenger list in the National Archives is add a sufficient amount of time onto the embarkation date for the vessel to cross the Atlantic—depending on whether she was a sailing vessel or steamship—and search the ship passenger lists of the port of arrival for that time period.

The Hamburg lists and the indexes to them are written in German handwriting, and contain many of the peculiarities described later in this text. Still, they are not prohibitively difficult to use. (For a detailed explanation of the lists and their indexes, see the article by Laraine K. Ferguson, or the work published by the Genealogical Department of The Church of Jesus Christ of Latter-day Saints, both cited in the bibliography.) However, searching the Hamburg lists for an ancestor's name requires that you bear in mind two crucial factors.

First, the lists are divided into two categories: *Listen Direkt* (Direct Lists) and *Listen Indirekt* (Indirect Lists). Direct lists enumerate passengers boarding ships that sailed directly to their destination without stopping at other ports. Indirect lists enumerate passengers boarding ships that stopped at an intermediate European or British port on the way to their final destination.

And second, prior to 1911, the Direct and Indirect Lists were bound and indexed separately. The Direct Lists of 1850 through 1854 have no index, because none is needed: the passengers are listed in alphabetical order by first letter of surname, so all names beginning with "A" are grouped together (but not in alphabetical order) for each of these years. For 1855 through 1910, each year has an alphabetical index (again, by first letter of surname only) for every ship, and the ships are indexed one after the other in chronological order of their departure from Hamburg. One index volume covers the lists of 1855 and 1856, another covers the lists of 1857 and 1858, another covers 1859 through 1861, and so on. For the Indirect Lists, 1855 through 1910, there is a single alphabetical index (by first letter of surname) for each year that covers all the ships that left that year. The index to the Indirect Lists comprises several volumes. Beginning with 1911 the two categories of lists—Direct and Indirect—were bound together and indexed together.

Let us say you are searching for your ancestor Heim Schwien. He was about fifty-four years old when he brought his family over from their native Germany. That was about 1856. You suspect that he sailed from the port of Hamburg.

First, you take the volume of the index to the Direct Lists that includes 1856, which happens to be Volume 8. You search through all the "S" surnames for the first "direct ship" that left Hamburg that year, then the second ship, then the third, and so forth. You come to "12/4 Elbe, Winzen n/New York" (12 April, ship *Elbe*, Captain Winzen, to New York), and find a Heim Schwien listed "m/frau u. kind." (with wife and children). The page reference is "79" (See illustration). This could be your ancestor.

Next, look at the Direct Lists for 1856—they happen to comprise Volume 10—and turn to page 79. There is the list of passengers boarding the ship *Elbe* under Captain Winzen, departing Hamburg on 12 April 1856, and destined for New York (See illustration). Heim Schwien, a fifty-four-year-old bridle maker from Heringsdorf, is listed with his wife Maria and four children. It is clear from all this data that you have the right family.

Estimating that it took a minimum of four weeks for the *Elbe* to cross the Atlantic, you begin your search of the passenger lists for the port of New York (micropublication M237) around mid-May. (Or, in this instance, since you are dealing with the port of New York, you might use M1066 to pinpoint the arrival date of the *Elbe*, and then turn to the lists on M237.) You come to the list of the bark *Elbe* and learn that it arrived on 21 May 1856 (See illustration). The Schwien family is there! Your search is over.

If you had not found your ancestor in the index to the *Direct* Lists, you would have proceeded to take the volume of the index to the *Indirect* Lists that covers 1856—which happens to be Volume 1—and search through all the "S" surnames for all of the "indirect ships" that left Hamburg in 1856.

Conducting a thorough search of the Hamburg lists, therefore, requires logic and concentration, and some familiarity with a few key German terms. But a small amount of practice leads to increased ease and competence in using this valuable resource, and may pay off in a big way—with the ship of your immigrant ancestor!

If, however, you prefer to have the Hamburg lists searched for you, write to the Historic Emigration Office, where staff members perform limited searches for a fee: Historic Emigration Office, c/o Tourist Information am Hafen, Bei den St.-Pauli-Landungsbrücken 3, P.O. Box 102249, D-2000 Hamburg 1, Germany. For excellent historical background on the experience of emigrating from Hamburg, visit <www.hamburg.de/LinkToYourRoots/english/welcome.htm>.

Le Havre Lists

No lists of passengers sailing out of Le Havre on passenger vessels are known to exist. However, the LDS Family History Library has a microfilm copy of records of passengers who sailed from Le Havre on board freight vessels from 1750 through 1886. The information about each passenger is extraordinary, including occupation and place of birth. Unfortunately, though, these departure manifests are very hard to read—the old French script is extremely fine and faint—and they are not indexed in any way.

European Passport Records

A resource closely related to emigration lists that may be used in a similar fashion for finding your ancestor's ship are European passport records. Many European countries have maintained records of passport applications submitted by prospective emigrants, and of passports granted to them. A manual about genealogical research in your ancestor's native country will address this topic. If you can discover a passport record for your ancestor, it will give you an idea of when he or she may have left the country.

How much time you allow between the granting of a passport and departure will vary widely from one period to another and from one locality to another. Consult the various works about the emigration pattern of your ancestor's national or ethnic or religious group referred to earlier in "Determining Your Ancestor's Probable Port of Departure."

Next, add to the approximate departure date the amount of time it would take to cross the Atlantic in that era (by sail and/or steam). This gives you an estimated arrival date. Then search for your ancestor's name in the ship passenger lists at the National Archives for that estimated arrival date.

This strategy helped me to find the 1830 arrival record of my ancestor, Nicholas Miller (referred to in the Introduction). Although there is a card for him in the *Index to Passenger Lists of Vessels Arriving at New York, NY, 1820–1846* (M261), his "Country of Origin" is indicated as "Switzerland." Knowing my forefather was from Lorraine,

Ship Passenger List. *This is from National Archives microfilm M237, Passenger Lists of Vessels Arriving at New York, 1820-1897, roll 162, May 15-June 9, 1856. Again, note Heim Schwien and family listed on lines 17-22.*

France, I ignored that card. (The WPA indexer did not err; on the list itself, Nicholas Miller and his entire clan are indicated as being from Switzerland. Indeed, every passenger on board is so indicated, causing me to blame a lazy ship's officer for the mistake.) But a footnote in a history of Lorrainian emigration to America stated that passport applications could be found in the Departmental Archives in Metz, Lorraine. So, estimating when Nicholas Miller would have applied for a passport, I sent for, and shortly thereafter received, a photocopy of the document: his passport had been granted on 17 February 1830. Based on scholarly studies of Lorrainian emigration of that era, I allowed four weeks for Nicholas Miller to sell his belongings and reach the port of Le Havre by train, and another eight weeks for him to cross the Atlantic. My search in the passenger lists of ships entering New York from Le Havre began with those of mid-May 1830, and I found the ship *Nile* arriving on the 24th—with the entire three-generation Miller family in steerage!

Using European passport records is neither as convenient nor as precise as using emigration lists. However, they are worth the effort when other strategies do not lead to success. Had I known that the winter of 1829-30 was unusually severe, and that the numerous Miller party had to wait a full week in Le Havre for the ice in the harbor to break up, my estimated arrival time would have been closer to reality.

If you do not know enough about your ancestor's immigration story to take advantage of any of the resources already discussed—book indexes, CD-ROM indexes, Internet websites, lists of vessels arriving in U.S. ports, emigration lists, and European passport records—use the sources described in "Where Can You Find This Information?" in the Introduction to secure additional facts. Accumulate specific facts until you have enough to pursue one of the suggested strategies, or until you are able to develop a strategy of your own. The other resources and information discussed in the following chapter may help.

Chapter Five

Other Resources and Information of Potential Value

This chapter examines materials and information that may be helpful for finding the arrival records of ancestors who immigrated under a variety of particular circumstances.

Crew Lists

Many American families treasure the oral tradition that their immigrant ancestor "worked his way over" as a member of the crew on a ship bound for the United States, or that the ancestor was a crew member who "jumped ship" when the vessel entered port. (The expression "jumped ship" means that the man entered the United States without legal documentation, not that he literally leapt from the deck of the vessel into the harbor!) For these families, crew lists on microfilm at the National Archives may help prove or disprove the tradition. There are crew lists for vessels arriving at:

- Boston, Mass.: 1917-1943
- Detroit, Mich.: 1946-1957
- Gloucester, Mass.: 1918-1943
- New Bedford, Mass.: 1917-1943
- New Orleans, La.: 1910-1945

- New York, N.Y.: 1897-1957
- San Francisco, Calif.: 1896-1954
- Seattle, Wash.: 1890-1957

These lists may contain the names of both American and alien seamen. The amount of information they provide about each crew member varies, but may include his length of service at sea, position in the ship's company, when and where he joined the vessel's crew, whether he was to be discharged at the port of arrival, and the seaman's age, race, nationality, height, weight, and literacy.

Unfortunately, the National Archives has no crew lists older than these. Some crew lists might possibly be found among the records of ship companies housed today in archives and libraries; locating them would therefore entail a search of repositories with manuscript collections. This is also true for the crew lists of merchant vessels, but if you know the name of the one on which your ancestor served, you could start your search at "Michael Palmer's List of Merchant Vessels" <www.geocities.com/mppraetorius>.

One final word about crew members on passenger ships and merchant vessels. It was not unusual for stowaways discovered en route to be impressed into service to earn their passage to America. On one passenger ship's list I found one male passenger's occupation given as "crew member."

Lists of Chinese Passengers

By the terms of the Chinese Exclusion Act of 1882 (See chapter 3), the U.S. government began keeping special lists of Chinese entering the country at the major West Coast ports. Today these lists are useful to Chinese Americans searching for ancestors' ships. The National Archives has the following lists on microfilm:

- Chinese laborers returning to the United States through port of San Francisco, 1882–1888
- Chinese passengers arriving at San Francisco, 1888–1914
- Chinese passengers applying for admission to the United States through port of San Francisco, 1903–1947
- Chinese passengers arriving at the port of Seattle (Port Townsend), 1882–1916
- Immigration and Naturalization Service case files of Chinese immigrants, Portland, Oregon, 1890–1914

Additional unmicrofilmed records may be found in the general Immigration and Naturalization Service records and in some National Archives Regional Archives.

Newspaper of the Port of Entry

Customs Passenger Lists were required by law to record the date when the ship entered the U.S. port, but not the date of departure from the foreign port. To learn when precisely your ancestors left their homeland, how much time they spent at sea, and what the conditions of the crossing were like, it may be necessary for you to consult a newspaper of the city where their ship docked. Newspapers of port cities usually had a column titled "Harbor News" or "Port Intelligence" or the like, which reported on vessels entering and departing the harbor. Information normally included the name, type, registry, and tonnage of the ship; the captain's name; for departing vessels, the port of destination; for arriving vessels, the port of origin, plus remarks about the weather and sea conditions of the passage, merchandise off-loaded, and passengers disembarked, including the names of all cabin passengers. Steerage passengers were accounted for in a global figure.

For example, the ship *Nile* (referred to earlier) sailed into New York Harbor on 24 May 1830. But the list does not give the date when the vessel left Le Havre. The *New York American* of 24 May 1830, indicates in its "Marine Journal" column that the "Ship Nile, Rockett, from Havre, sailed evening of the 4th of April." The captain was John Rockett, the port of departure, Le Havre. The notice goes on to state that the *Nile* brought merchandise for Jones & Megrath, names nine cabin passengers, and concludes that there were "120 in steerage." It was from the newspaper item, therefore, that I learned that it took my ancestors seven weeks and two days to cross the Atlantic. This, in turn, allowed me to investigate weather conditions in Le Havre in late March and early April 1830. The winter of 1829–30 was particularly long and severe, and that the ice in the harbor was late in breaking, indicating that the *Nile* was one of the first ships to sail.

The arrival of the sailing vessel that brought George F. Ring to America (mentioned in "Published Book Indexes" earlier) is described this way in the "Marine Intelligence" column of the *New York Daily Times* of 21 May 1853: "Ship South America (of Boston), Lincoln, Havre, 36 ds., ballast and 445 passengers to master. Experienced heavy weather. Carried away foremast. Had 4 deaths." Lincoln was the captain, Le Havre was the port of origin, and the departure date may be calculated to have been 15 April 1853. More noteworthy than these statistics, however, is the notation that the *South America* had weathered a tempest so violent that the forward-most of the ship's three masts had collapsed and four people had died. As no deaths are recorded on the passenger list, it is reasonable to conclude that the unfortunate persons who lost their lives were crew members, perhaps aloft on the mast when it toppled into the raging ocean.

The sample case explained in chapter 2 showed that Ignazio Colletta arrived in New Orleans from Palermo on the SS. *Trinacria* on 9 June 1890. That list, too, lacked the date of departure. But an item in *The Daily Picayune—New Orleans* titled "Immigrants from Italy," which appeared on Tuesday, 10 June 1890, provides not only the date of departure—14 May 1890—but also detailed information about the size and ownership of the SS. *Trinacria*, her entire itinerary (she had called at three intermediate ports), an account of weather conditions at each of those points along the route, and the remark that the *Trinacria* carried "fruit and 450 Italian immigrants."

Newspapers will report anything unusual about the arrival of your ancestor's ship, such as whether it was detained in quarantine because of a threat of contagious disease. That happened to the SS. *Veendam* in 1892, with the Schnell family on board; for their story, see "Conclusion: Ellis Island—What's Myth? What's Reality?" Such information complements the statistics you find in the list, "filling in" the fuller story of your ancestor's immigration.

Immigration via Canada

During most of the nineteenth century the United States government kept no record of immigrants arriving overland from Canada. The first immigration inspection stations along the Canadian border were established by a Congressional act of 1891, because by that time about forty percent of the passengers arriving in Canada were bound for the United States.

In 1895 the United States and Canada established a joint inspection system. Passengers arriving in Canada who declared their intention to proceed to the United States were inspected by U.S. officials at the Canadian port of entry and enumerated on U.S. immigration lists. Halifax, Nova Scotia, and Montreal and Quebec City, Quebec, were the major East Coast ports at that time, and Victoria and Vancouver, British Columbia, were the major West Coast ports. Besides being named on U.S. lists, arriving immigrants were issued inspection cards that they surrendered to U.S. officials on board the

The card for Thomas P. Boland from National Archives micropublication M1461, Soundex Index to Canadian Border Entries through the St. Albans, VT, District, 1895-1924, roll #39, reveals an extensive amount of detailed information about the young man's life and travels.

trains as they crossed the border. Two sets of records, therefore, were created regarding immigrants arriving via Canada: passenger lists and compiled inspection cards. The lists are almost identical to the Immigration Passenger Lists described previously, i.e., they contain a substantial amount of personal information about every individual enumerated on them. The surrendered inspection cards contain only essential immigration information in abbreviated form.

These "Canadian Border Crossing" records were microfilmed by the Immigration and Naturalization Service in the 1950s as five micropublications, M1461 through M1465. Together they cover the period 1895 through 1954, and almost all of them are indexed by individual passenger name. Unfortunately, large portions of the indexes are illegible due to deterioration, and the original index cards were destroyed after the filming was completed. These publications may be viewed at the National Archives, Regional Archives, LDS Family

History Library and worldwide Family History Centers, and some public libraries with extensive genealogical collections.

It is important to note that prior to 30 September 1906, theses records do not include Canadians entering the United States, but only non-Canadians; after that date, both Canadians and non-Canadians are included. For complete information about these microfilms, visit the National Archives website at <www.nara.gov> or read the article by Constance Potter cited in the bibliography.

For information about Canadian passenger arrival records, visit the website of the National Archives of Canada at <www.archives.ca>. In brief, there are very few lists of immigrants arriving in Canada prior to 1865. Perhaps the major resource is the "Miscellaneous Immigration Index," which lists mostly immigrants from the British Isles to Quebec and Ontario, 1801–1849 (accessible at <www.ingeneas.com/free/main.html>). For the years 1865 through 1935, however, much more informative arrival lists are kept in the National Archives of Canada, located in Ottawa, Ontario, and all of these are available on microfilm. Unfortunately, they are not indexed, except for Quebec arrivals from 1865 through 1869 (an old card index of questionable accuracy) and Halifax arrivals from 1881 and 1882, both of which indexes have been microfilmed. A transcription of the immigration records of 1925 through 1935 is easily searchable online at the National Archives of Canada website.

Immigration via Mexico

Records of people entering the United States across the Mexican border from about 1903 through 1955, which are in the custody of the Immigration and Naturalization Service, are currently being microfilmed and deposited in the National Archives. Rather than lists, these records are individual cards, and they comprise "card manifests" for twenty-two border crossing stations in Arizona, California, New

Mexico, and Texas. Many of the records are arranged alphabetically; others are arranged chronologically, then by manifest number, and these usually have an alphabetical index.

Note that prior to 30 September 1906, theses records do not include Mexicans entering the United States, but only non-Mexicans; after that date, both Mexicans and non-Mexicans are included. For more detailed information about these records of immigration via Mexico, including the micropublication numbers for each border crossing station, visit the National Archives website <www.nara. gov> or read the series of articles by Clare Prechtel-Klustins cited in the bibliography.

U.S. Departure Records

Records of passengers departing U.S. ports are close to nonexistent. Except for a few lists of American citizens traveling overseas during a portion of the War of 1812 (R.G. 59, General Records of the Department of State), no U.S. departure records prior to 1895 are known to exist. Beginning in that year, rare departures may sometimes be found interfiled in the Canadian border crossing records for Canaan and St. Albans, Vermont; and beginning about 1903, a few rare departures may be found interfiled in the Mexican border crossing records.

In 1917 the Immigration and Naturalization Service began recording departures at U.S. ports, but these records were not kept permanently. Consequently, only a miniscule amount of departure information, 1926–1952, is available (consult the *Guide to Genealogical Research in the National Archives of the United States*, pp. 62-63.)

Peter E. Carr is currently compiling *San Francisco Passenger Departure Lists* (San Bernardino, Calif.: Cuban Index, 1991-date) from sources other than federal records. So far he has published five volumes covering 30 September 1850 through 31 December 1852.

U.S. passport applications (discussed under "Civil and Religious Records" in chapter 1) sometimes contain a general statement as to when the applicant intended to travel overseas.

Other than these scant sources, there are no U.S. departure records.

Immigration Laws of 1921 and 1924

The Emergency Quota Act was passed by the U.S. Congress and signed by President Harding on 19 May 1921. It established for the first time in American history, not just stricter regulations for admitting aliens into the United States—that kind of law had been passed earlier, as noted in chapters 2 and 3—but *numerical quotas* for immigration. This was what many European and Japanese families had feared: families were split by an ocean, with no idea of when, if ever, they would be reunited.

The Emergency Quota Act was called "emergency" legislation because it had been instigated by panicked American workers who worried about the ever-rising tide of poor, uneducated European and Japanese laborers flooding the United States work force. The American workers maintained that the immigrants undercut their salaries or deprived them of their livelihoods altogether. The "National Origins Formula" of this law was calculated to be strictest against southern and eastern Europeans and the Japanese, who constituted the majority of immigrants in the years just prior to World War I.

The Emergency Quota Act was intended as a temporary measure—expiring on 30 June 1922—to allow Congress sufficient time to debate the immigration issue and legislate a definitive resolution to the problem. But the issue was controversial and perplexing, the problems personal and emotional, the debate heated and protracted. Congress needed more time. So the law was extended for two additional years, to expire 30 June 1924.

Many Europeans, though, could not wait. Rumors spread through the towns and villages of Southern and Eastern Europe that America would admit no more immigrants; or that men could immigrate but not women; or that men already in the United States could stay but could never be joined by their spouses and children.

Many desperate Europeans were ready to take drastic steps. Southern and eastern Europeans flocked to northern European ports to book passage on northern European vessels. Somehow, this stratagem worked. You may discover that a southern or eastern European ancestor who came to the United States between 1921 and 1924 left Europe from Liverpool, Le Havre, or Bremen.

Congress finally legislated a complex set of rules to allow for the unification of separated alien families, in certain cases and under certain circumstances. The complex stipulations were contained in the Immigration Act signed into law by President Coolidge on 21 May 1924. Visas—another "first" in American history—became a requirement for entry into the United States. By requiring that emigrants be approved for admission into the United States before leaving their native lands, Congress put an end to the practice—common before 1924—of turning away unacceptable immigrants at the American port of arrival and sending them home. Thousands of Europeans and Japanese got their numbers and began to wait their turn. This new legislation, however, was of little concern to the many Europeans who had managed to make it into the United States through the "back door" of Northern Europe.

Obtaining a Picture of Your Ancestor's Ship

Three museums devoted to the history of seafaring and ships may supply more information about, and possibly a picture of, your ancestor's sailing vessel or steamship:

- Mystic Seaport Museum, 50 Greenmanville Avenue, Mystic, CT 06355-0990 or www.mysticseaport.org

• Peabody Essex Museum, East India Square, Salem, MA 01970 or www.pem.org

• Mariners Museum, 100 Museum Drive, Newport News, VA 23606 or www.mariner.org

Mystic Seaport Museum has the most extensive collection of materials relating to sailing ships; Peabody Essex Museum and Mariners Museum hold more materials relating to steamships. The vast majority of sailing ship materials in all three museums pertains to nineteenth-century vessels. For earlier periods, you must rely on books about ships in your local public library, as discussed in chapter 2, "Learning More about Your Ancestor's Sailing Vessel."

The Steamship Historical Society of America

The Steamship Historical Society of America is a national organization of individuals interested in the history of steamships, both freight and passenger, from the earliest ones of the 1830s through those of the twentieth century. Its extensive collection of books, manuscripts, and steamship memorabilia is conserved in the Steamship Historical Society of America Collection, Ann House, Librarian, Langsdale Library, University of Baltimore, 1420 Maryland Avenue, Baltimore, Maryland 21201-7790. (The telephone number is (410) 837-4334, but no search requests are accepted by phone, FAX, or e-mail.)

The collection does not include any original passenger lists, but it does include over 200,000 engravings, drawings, photographs, and postcards of steamships. Once you know the name of the ship that brought your ancestor to the United States, you may have the collection searched for a picture of it. If there is one in the collection, the society will have a copy made for a nominal fee. The society can also provide technical information about particular steamships, such as registry, tonnage, year of construction, and so forth. So you may learn a lot about your ancestor's ship even if you cannot find a picture of her.

The website of the Steamship Historical Society <www.sshsa.net/index.html> links to its collection <www.ubalt.edu/archives/ship/ship.htm>, where a sampling of the many ships for which the society has images is posted. For example, if we search for the SS. *Augusta Victoria*, the vessel that brought Christoph Mueller to the United States from Hamburg in 1891, we will find that the Steamship Historical Society does have an 1889 photograph of this ship. All we have to do now is fill in the form provided on the website and mail it with a check to the University of Baltimore.

In addition, the bibliography at the end of this volume contains several works that provide information about, and photographs of, steamships that brought our forebears to the United States. Also, on the Internet, *Kinshipsprints* <www.kinshipsprints.com> offers reproductions of prints of over 300 steamships, mostly postcards, which may be ordered online.

Conclusion

Ellis Island:
What's Myth? What's Reality?

Ellis Island occupies a "mythical" place in the history of the United States and rightly so. Millions of Americans trace their ancestry to immigrants who arrived at Ellis Island. However, it is equally true that millions of Americans trace their ancestry to immigrants who did not arrive at Ellis Island—though their descendants today may think they did! Many myths and misconceptions about Ellis Island persist in popular American thought, undermining the research endeavors and family history reporting of numerous genealogists. Why did many thousands of immigrants who came through the port of New York never set foot on Ellis Island? During what years was the inspection station in New York Harbor not Ellis Island, but Castle Garden? Were names really changed arbitrarily by Ellis Island immigration officials? Was the process really so horrific? The following information may help put Ellis Island in its proper place within the larger context of U.S. immigration history, and set the record straight regarding what is fact and what is myth.

Dates of Immigrant Processing

No Immigrant Receiving Stations: 1624—31 July 1855
In colonial times, as noted in chapter 1, numerous ports were used by immigrant settlers, and there were no receiving stations at all to

process them. Even in the nineteenth and twentieth centuries, as chapter 3 has shown, immigrants to the United States arrived at many minor ports—including the oft-forgotten Pacific Coast ports of San Francisco, Seattle, and Port Townsend—in addition to the five major ports—Boston, New York, Philadelphia, Baltimore, and New Orleans. Furthermore, chapter 5 made clear that thousands of immigrants arrived by land, too, via Canada and Mexico.

Castle Garden: 1 August 1855—18 April 1890

The State of New York founded this country's first center for examining and processing arriving immigrants in 1855. It was established in Castle Garden, a former music hall on an island off the southwest tip of Manhattan, which was owned by the city of New York and leased to the Board of Commissioners of Emigration of the State of New York. (The circular, red stone foundation of Castle Garden stands today in Battery Park; it surrounds the office where tickets to the Ellis Island museum are sold.) One purpose for the facility was to help health officials prevent people with contagious diseases from entering the country. But it was also hoped that a receiving station located off the mainland would serve to relieve the horrors—fraud, robbery, deceit, kidnapping—that afflicted immigrants the moment they stepped onto land. Practical assistance, information, and direction were also provided the new arrivals. Castle Garden was a giant step forward in the humane reception of immigrants to the United States.

Beginning in 1875 (See chapter 3) the processing of immigrants was handled jointly by state and federal officials. This arrangement, often contentious, lasted fifteen years. Then, on 18 April 1890, the Secretary of the Treasury terminated the contract his department held with the Board of Commissioners of Emigration of the State of New York, and assumed total control of immigration affairs at the harbor. But the city of New York refused to allow the federal government the use of Castle Garden. Castle Garden's career as an immigrant receiving station ended.

Barge Office: 19 April 1890—31 December 1891

The following day—19 April 1890—the U.S. government established a temporary processing center in the old Barge Office at the southeast foot of Manhattan near the old U.S. Customs House. (Both buildings are long gone; today the terminal for the Staten Island Ferry occupies the approximate site). About 525,000 immigrants were processed through the old Barge Office during the one year and eight months it served this purpose.

Ellis Island: 1 January 1892—14 June 1897

Meanwhile, the U.S. government handed over to the Secretary of the Treasury a small, low, swampy piece of federal property situated in New York Harbor called Ellis Island. This was to be the site of the country's first *federal* immigrant processing station. After substantial enlargement of the site, the Ellis Island facility was built and opened 1 January 1892. Note that if your ancestors arrived in New York *anytime prior to 1892*, they clearly did not go through Ellis Island!

The original Ellis Island edifice was cavernous and hailed by government officials and the public alike as a modern marvel. Constructed entirely of wood, it was three stories high and had lots of windows for light and air. It was designed to "easily" handle up to 10,000 immigrants a day. In 1891, as Ellis Island was rising, the federal government assumed total jurisdiction over immigration affairs at all ports, not just New York. Federal immigrant processing centers eventually appeared in other ports as well, among them Locust Point in Baltimore Harbor, Angel Island in San Francisco Bay, and Galveston Island at Galveston.

Ellis Island: What's Myth? What's Reality?

Just when the United States was poised and ready to take on the onslaught of immigrants, immigration dropped off abruptly. Cholera broke out in European ports in August 1892. Then the U.S. economy slipped into a long period of depression that lasted for years.

On 14 June 1897, "just before midnight," fire broke out in the state-of-the-art, all-wooden building on Ellis Island, and it burned to the ground. All administrative records for Castle Garden, 1855-1890, and most records retained from the old Barge Office and Ellis Island, 1890–1897, were lost. However—contrary to persistent hearsay—no ship passenger lists were destroyed, for they were kept elsewhere in the custody of what were then called the Bureau of Customs and the Bureau of Immigration.

Barge Office: 15 June 1897–16 December 1900

Following the destruction of the Ellis Island facility, the old Barge Office was reactivated as a processing center. It was used as such for three and a half years while the new Ellis Island building was being erected.

Ellis Island: 17 December 1900—1924

On 17 December 1900, the new building on Ellis Island—constructed of steel, brick and stone, and hoped to be fireproof—opened. Note, therefore, that if your ancestors arrived in New York between 15 June 1897 and 16 December 1900, they did not go through Ellis Island!

Though fireproof, the new processing facility was much too small from the start and would have to be expanded many times. Immigration statistics had been depressed through the 1890s, and the new station had been designed to accommodate far fewer numbers of immigrants than the old one since officials thought the peak years of immigration had passed!

It is also important to remember that cabin passengers—that is, first and second class passengers—did not pass through Ellis Island. A U.S. Health Service boat would approach the ocean liner as it sailed into New York Harbor, and a doctor and nurse would come aboard to perform a cursory inspection of passengers in cabins. After the steamer docked at a Manhattan pier, only steerage passengers—toting all their belongings—would board ferries that took them back out into the harbor to Ellis Island for their legal inspection and health inspection.

Summary of Dates

To summarize, here is the chronology of immigrant processing at the port of New York:

1624—31 July 1855	no receiving station
1 Aug 1855—18 Apr 1890	Castle Garden
19 April 1890—31 Dec 1891	Barge Office
1 Jan 1892—14 Jun 1897	Ellis Island
15 Jun 1897—16 Dec 1900	Barge Office
17 Dec 1900—1924	Ellis Island

What this historical sketch demonstrates is that thousands of immigrants who arrived in New York, cabin class and steerage, never set foot on Ellis Island—not even during the years when the federal receiving facility was in operation. Take this into account, therefore, before you claim your ancestors arrived at Ellis Island!

When the Immigration Act became law in 1924 (discussed in chapter 5), requiring visas and providing for the inspection of prospective immigrants at U.S. embassies overseas, Ellis Island lost its *raison d'être*. It closed that year as an immigrant receiving station. For thirty years it was used, on and off, as a detention and deportation center. Finally, on 29 November 1954, Ellis Island was locked and abandoned, and placed on the U.S. government's excess property list.

Frequently Asked Questions

How Many People Passed through Ellis Island?

So, ultimately, how many people really passed through Ellis Island? Figures vary widely among published sources. Works cited in Section VIII of the Bibliography titled "Ellis Island" estimate that while the facility was operating as an immigrant receiving station—1892 through 1924—seventeen million men, women, and children passed through its doors.

That may be true, but the figure is misleading. It is presumably based on the total number of names appearing on the ship passenger lists for the port of New York during those years. But a substantial number of the passengers named on those lists returned two, three, or more times; many others did not remain in the United States permanently; and many others, as noted, did not undergo processing at Ellis Island.

A second source gives an even greater number. The *American Family Immigration History Center* <www.ellisislandrecords.org> states: "Between 1892 and 1924 over twenty-two million passengers and members of ships' crews came through Ellis Island and the port of New York." That figure, obviously, includes crew members as well as passengers who entered the port of New York, those who underwent processing at Ellis Island as well as those who did not.

Taking into account all the variables, statisticians estimate that roughly twelve million immigrants who became permanent residents of the United States passed through Ellis Island.

Did Immigration Officials Change Names?

Did indifferent immigration officials change anybody's name

because they could not understand it or pronounce it? No! This is one of the most widespread and oft-repeated myths about Ellis Island. Without a doubt, the surnames of many immigrants were changed around the time of arrival in America or shortly thereafter; but the change was effected due to a variety of causes other than callous U.S. government officers.

One reason that passenger lists were expanded by law in 1893 (discussed in chapter 3) was so that the "Inspector [in the immigrant receiving center] had in his hands a written record of the immigrant he was inspecting and, asking the same questions over again, could compare the oral statements with it." The inspectors, therefore, read the names already written down on the lists, and they had at their service a large staff of translators who worked alongside them in the Great Hall of the Ellis Island facility.

U.S. immigration officials did not—as popular American myth persistently claims—arbitrarily and cavalierly change any immigrant's name!

How Bad Was the Ellis Island Experience?

For the millions who did endure processing at Ellis Island, was it really so bad? Certainly not as bad as coming to America during the age of long and difficult sail passage. Novels and movies tend to overdramatize and sentimentalize the Ellis Island experience. Scholars estimate that the vast majority of immigrants passed through the legal and health inspections and departed the island within three hours.

By the time Ellis Island started operation in 1892, migrating to the United States was an established and familiar procedure. Rare was the European who did not know someone who had made the journey and returned to tell about it (as did the "birds of passage" mentioned in chapter 3), or who had not heard lengthy emigrant letters read aloud to gatherings of neighbors. Steamships, even steerage accommodations, offered amenities unimaginable on sailing vessels, and they crossed the Atlantic in much less time.

No doubt, the immigrants passing through inspection at Ellis Island suffered some anxiety and disorientation; their personal recollections captured on audiotape and retained in the American Family Immigration History Center on Ellis Island attest to this. They were being "judged," and they worried that the American officials might find them wanting. But they knew what was coming before they left their homeland, they had been forewarned, and the procedure, for most, was concluded with surprising dispatch.

On occasion, extraordinary circumstances made getting into America a tedious experience, as it was for Franz and Marianna Schnell and their nine children in the late summer of 1892. By August of that year, news of the spread of cholera through Russia and many cities of central Europe—even Hamburg!—had reached the United States, so steamships arriving from northern European ports

Schnell Family 1897. Photo courtesy Jerry Schnell.

were barred from entering U.S. ports. Ships headed for New York were required to dock at Swinburne Island or Hoffman Island outside the Verrazano Narrows and raise the quarantine flag. The Schnell family, Germans from Russia, were traveling on board the SS. *Veendam*, out of Rotterdam, and on 30 August 1892, they docked at Hoffman Island.

When their turn came (there were several ships ahead of them) the passengers of the *Veendam* were disembarked and ushered through a process that entailed stripping, showering with plenty of soap, and the disinfecting of all their clothing and baggage. This completed—it normally took three to four hours—the Schnells were returned to their ship. Only after U.S. Health Service officials determined that there was no threat of contagion—three days, in this case—was the *Veendam* allowed to lower the quarantine flag, enter the harbor, and dock at a Manhattan pier. From there, steerage passengers—the eleven Schnells among them—proceeded out to Ellis Island for their

SS. **Veendam**. *Photo courtesy Jerry Schnell.*

legal and health inspections. Though unexpected and trying, the immigration experience of the Schnells and their fellow travelers ended happily, for no cholera had been found on the SS. *Veendam*. Passengers aboard other steamers docked at quarantine that August and September of 1892—particularly the SS. *Moravia*, on which twenty-two steerage passengers died—were less fortunate.

Ellis Island's Place in U.S. Immigration History

Ellis Island's mythical place in U.S. immigration history is well deserved. In sheer numbers of passenger arrivals, it looms far beyond other major and minor ports. That preeminence should not be diminished by dispelling the many myths and misunderstandings that cling to the collective American imagination. On the contrary, the reality of Ellis Island is more than enough to inspire awe and appreciation! Read more fascinating facts and figures in the works cited in Section VIII of the bibliography, "Ellis Island."

Closing Comments

Despite all the published, microfilmed, and digitized passenger lists, despite all the indexes, search engines, and research aids, despite all of the instruction and helpful hints provided in this manual, you may still not find the ship that brought your immigrant ancestor to America. Success in any genealogical endeavor cannot be guaranteed. As stated at the outset, many of the old lists have been lost or destroyed, many that have survived remain unindexed, and even the indexes that do exist contain numerous inaccurately transcribed names, rendering those passengers, too, as good as unindexed.

This small book does not describe every resource available for conducting your search, or explain every possible methodology. The bibliography is selective and representative, not exhaustive. The examples, too, are representative. You must analyze your research problem and find the works most helpful to you. Remember, every immigrant ancestor's story is unique, so every search for an ancestor's ship is unique. What this manual provides is a *guide* to finding the arrival record you seek.

As you search, you will gain increasing familiarity with the indexes and the lists. You will become attuned to their peculiarities and you will appreciate their riches. So even if your research path does not lead to your immigrant ancestor's ship, the search itself will be enlightening. For it will lead you to appreciate fully what it means that they came in ships, the Europeans, Africans, Asians who arrived in America from the late sixteenth century through the mid-twentieth century, the hundreds, the thousands, the millions who came. They came in ships.

BIBLIOGRAPHIC NOTE

This manual contains numerous statements of fact, yet cites no sources for them. Here is the explanation. *They Came in Ships* originated in 1989 as a slim guide intended primarily for visitors to the newly opened immigration museum on Ellis Island. As such, documentation was considered unnecessary. The information it contained was drawn from the author's years of reading and teaching in the subject area of National Archives passenger arrival records and the American immigration experience generally. As use of the manual increased among genealogists, it was expanded but, once again, specific source citation was considered extraneous, as the Select Bibliography at the end was both extensive and annotated.

Today, the importance of documentation is being stressed within the field of genealogy. Besides conferring credibility on the genealogical work, proper documentation allows users to consult the sources the author has consulted. Nevertheless, to provide source notes for *They Came in Ships* at this stage in its life would be a tedious task of dubious value, for the reader interested in delving more deeply into the subject matter may still use the enlarged and updated Select Bibliography to do so.

To help readers access key works on the various aspects of passenger arrival records and the American immigrant experience, the Select Bibliography is broken down into topic categories. Most of the cited works contain notes and a bibliography, or at least an informative preface or introduction, for readers interested in pursuing a more scholarly investigation of the topic. The corpus of published literature about U.S. passenger arrival records and the American immigration experience is colossal and continually growing, hence the use of the term "select." For additional pertinent resources the reader is referred to the substantial bibliographies in *The Source, A Guidebook of American Genealogy*, chapter 13, "Immigration: Finding Immigrant Origins," and also *Printed Sources, A Guide to Published Genealogical Records*, "Immigration Sources," chapter 14. These, together with the Select Bibliography which follows, should constitute a more than adequate entrée into the vast realm intimated in *They Came in Ships*.

Select Bibliography

Records Descriptions and Research Aids

Colletta, John Philip. "New York Passenger Arrival Records, 1846-1897." Audiotape of lecture, F-80: Repeat Performance <www.audiotapes.com>, 1999. Strategies for finding the ship of an ancestor who arrived in New York during unindexed years.

Cyndi's List of Genealogy Sites on the Internet <www.cyndislist.com/ships.htm> links to numerous sites with information about ships, passenger lists, and crew lists: libraries, archives & museums; mailing lists, newsgroups & chat rooms; professional researchers, volunteers & other research services; publications, microfilm & microfiche; shipwrecks; and societies & groups. (When using the Internet, always look for the source of the information, then access the original record to confirm accuracy! The Internet is rife with error.)

Family History Library, Salt Lake City, Utah, has on microfilm many records of passengers arriving at American ports, as well as records of passengers departing from European ports, which may be borrowed and viewed at Family History Centers worldwide. Search the FHL catalog at <www.familysearch.org>.

"Immigration Records" is an informative essay at the World Wide Web site of the National Archives, <http://www.nara.gov/genealogy/immigration/immigrat.html>.

Konecny, Lawrence H. "Galveston's Missing Passenger Lists." *FORUM*, the journal of the Federation of Genealogical Societies, vol. 6, no. 2 (summer 2001): 1, 13–14. In-depth discussion of what records are and are not available for Galveston.

Krasner-Khait, Barbara. "If Not Through New York, Then Where?" *Family Chronicle*, March/April 2000: 9–11. Discussion of other ports of entry and why immigrants used them.

Meyerink, Kory L. "Immigration Sources." Chapter 14 in *Printed Sources: A Guide to Published Genealogical Records*. Salt Lake City: Ancestry, 1998. Thorough overview of published passenger arrival information.

_____, and Loretto Dennis Szucs. "Immigration: Finding Immigrant Origins." Chapter 13 in *The Source: A Guidebook of American Genealogy*, rev. ed. Salt Lake City: Ancestry, Inc., 1997. Superb discussion of resources and methods for tracing immigrant ancestors in the United States and country of origin.

Mokotoff, Gary. "Strategies for Using the Ellis Island Database." *FORUM*, the journal of the Federation of Genealogical Societies, vol. 13, no. 3 (fall 2001): 17–20. Detailed discussion of the strong points and weaknesses of the website of the American Family Immigration History Center.

National Archives Trust Fund Board. *Guide to Genealogical Research in the National Archives*, rev. ed. Washington, D.C.: NATF, 2000. Chapter 2, "Passenger Arrivals and Border Crossings," provides a thorough description of the various kinds of arrival lists and the indexes to them.

_____. *Immigrant and Passenger Arrivals: A Select Catalog of National Archives Microfilm Publications*, rev. ed. Washington, D.C.: NATF, 1991. Roll-by-roll catalog of microfilmed lists and indexes. For each micropublication whose title begins with the letter "M" (e.g., M1066) there is a Descriptive Pamphlet that gives an account of the records on the microfilm.

Potter, Constance. "St. Albans Passenger Arrival Records." *Prologue: Journal of the National Archives* 22, no. 1 (spring 1990): 90-93. Describes National Archives records of immigration across the Canadian border, 1895–1954, and their indexes.

Prechtel-Kluskens, Claire. "Mexican Border Crossing Records." *NGS Newsmagazine.* "Part 1: How and Why Immigration Records Were Collected," May/June 1999, pp. 156–159; "Part 2: The Information Collected," July/August 1999, pp. 182–183; "Part 3, "Available Microfilm Publications," September/October 1999, pp. 278–281.

Remington, Gordon L. "Feast or Famine: Problems in the Genealogical Use of *The Famine Immigrants* and *Germans to America.*" *National Genealogical Society Quarterly* 78, no. 2 (June 1990): 135-146. Superb critique of these two sets of published abstracts of U.S. passenger arrival records.

Smith, Marian L. "The Creation and Destruction of Ellis Island Immigration Manifests." *Prologue, Journal of the National Archives* 28, no. 3 (fall 1996): 240–245; and no. 4 (winter 1996): 314–318. In-depth study of Immigration Passenger Lists for the port of New York.

_____. "Immigration through Great Lakes Ports of Entry, 1895–1955." Audiotape of lecture, S–148: Repeat Performance <www.audiotapes.com>, 1998.

A Supplemental Index to Passenger Lists of Vessels Arriving at Atlantic and Gulf Coast Ports, 1820–1874. National Archives Micropublication M334. Contains some pre-1848 Boston passenger arrivals and some pre-1853 New Orleans passenger arrivals, thus supplementing the indexes for those ports. Also contains arrivals at all other major ports except New York and about 60 minor ports.

Tepper, Michael H. *American Passenger Arrival Records: A Guide to the Records of Immigrants Arriving at American Ports by Sail and Steam*, rev. ed. Baltimore: Genealogical Publishing Co., 1993. Thorough overview not only of ship lists, but other types of records that provide immigrant arrival information. Important bibliography.

Wittke, Carl F. *We Who Built America: The Saga of the Immigrant*, rev. ed. Cleveland: Western Reserve University Press, 1964. Scholarly account of migration by period and national group, including information about which ports were used by which immigrants.

Published Arrival Lists and Indexes

American Family Immigration History Center <www.ellisislandrecords. org> contains digitized images of the passenger arrival records of New York, 1892–1924, and a search engine for finding passengers among the estimated twenty-two million names.

Avakian, Linda L. *Armenian Immigrants: Boston, 1891–1901; New York, 1880–1897*. Camden, Me.: Picton Press, 1996. These abstracted lists with an index fill gaps in National Archives indexes to Boston and New York.

Baca, Leo. *Czech Immigration Passenger Lists*. 9 vols. Richardson, Tex.: Old Homestead Publishing Co., 1983–2000. Czech arrivals at various U.S. ports, 1847–1899, extracted from lists in the National Archives.

Bentley, Elizabeth P. *Passenger Arrivals at the Port of New York, 1820–1829: From Customs Passenger Lists*. Baltimore: Genealogical Publishing Co., 1999. This alphabetical index of over 85,000 names is based on the original microfilmed lists; it is not a mere transcription of the National Archives index.

Select Bibliography

Boyer, Carl, ed. *Ship Passenger Lists.* 4 vols. Newhall, Calif.: 1977–80. Indexes numerous published ship lists: vol. 1, National and New England, 1600-1825; vol. 2, New York and New Jersey, 1600-1825; vol. 3, The South, 1538–1825; and vol. 4, Pennsylvania and Delaware, 1641–1825.

Cassady, Michael. *New York Passenger Arrivals, 1849–1868.* Papillion, Neb.: Nimmo, 1983. Thirty-three selected lists naming about 10,200 persons.

D'Addezio, Illya James. *D'Addezio.com* <www.daddezio.com> links to several hundred ship passenger lists posted on the Internet. However, beware of third- and fourth-hand materials! Always look for source of information, then access original record to confirm accuracy.

Filby, P. William, *et al.*, eds. *Passenger and Immigration Lists Index: A Guide to Published Arrival Records of More Than 3,806,000 Passengers Who Came to the New World between the Sixteenth and the Twentieth Centuries.* Detroit: Gale Research Co., 1981–present. Originally 3 vols. Supplemental volumes published annually and gathered every few years into "cumulative supplements." (Available on CD-ROM #354 by Genealogy.com.) Contains millions of names appearing in published ship lists and other types of published arrival records.

Galveston County Genealogical Society. *Ships Passenger Lists, Port of Galveston, Texas, 1846–1871.* Easley, S.C.: Southern Historical Press, 1984. Over 9,000 names.

German and Swiss Settlers in America, 1700s-1800s. CD-ROM #267 by Genealogical Publishing Company and Genealogy.com. Includes immigrant names from seventeen books published previously in paper form.

Glazier, Ira A., ed. *The Famine Immigrants: Lists of Irish Immigrants Arriving at the Port of New York, 1846–1851.* 7 vols. Baltimore: Genealogical Publishing Co., 1983–86. Since New York arrivals of 1847–1896 are not indexed at the National Archives, this is a very helpful work.

_____. *Migration from the Russian Empire: Lists of Passengers Arriving at the Port of New York.* 6 vols. Baltimore: Genealogical Publishing Co., 1995. Ongoing. So far, covers 1875-1891. Includes Jews (43 percent of total), Poles, Lithuanians, Finns, Germans, and Russians.

_____, and P. William Filby, eds. *Germans to America: Lists of Passengers Arriving at U.S. Ports.* Wilmington, Del.: Scholarly Resources, Inc., 1988-present. 63 vols. Ongoing. (Years 1850-74 available on CD-ROM #355, and years 1875–88 available on CD-ROM #356, both by Genealogy.com.) For 1850–55, reproduces entire lists of ships with a minimum of eighty percent German surnames. For 1856–92, lists only those passengers identified as "German" on all ships, regardless of national percentages on board. Indexed. (Numerous errors; use with caution.)

_____. *Italians to America: Lists of Passengers Arriving at U.S. Ports, 1880–1899.* Wilmington, Del.: Scholarly Resources, Inc., 1992-present. 12 vols. Ongoing. So far, all passengers are New York arrivals; other ports will follow.

Haury, David A., ed. *Index to Mennonite Immigrants on U.S. Passenger Lists, 1872–1904* North Newton, Kans.: Mennonite Library and Archives, 1986. Nearly 15,000 Mennonite passengers, mostly Germans from Russia, in chronological order of ship arrival.

Hill, Georgie A. "Passenger Arrivals at Salem and Beverly, Mass., 1798-1800." *New England Historical and Genealogical Register* 106 (July 1952): 203–209. Transcribes nine original passenger lists found in Record Group 36 at the National Archives.

Holcomb, Brent H. *Passenger Arrivals at the Port of Charleston, 1820–1829.* Baltimore: Genealogical Publishing Co., 1994. Compiled from copies of original Customs Passenger Lists prepared by the Collector of Customs for the State Department and Transcripts prepared by the State Department for its quarterly reports to Congress. No original lists, or other federal arrival records, exist for Charleston.

Immigrant Ships Transcribers Guild (http://istg.rootsweb.com) is a group of volunteers who are transcribing passenger arrival records and up-loading them to the Internet. Selection of ships is still very small and selective, but easily searched.

Immigrants to America, 17th–19th Century. CD-ROM #352 by Genealogical Publishing Company and Genealogy.com. Includes immigrant names from a wide variety of books covering different national groups in different places.

Immigrants to Pennsylvania, 1680s–1770s. CD-ROM #501 by Genealogical Publishing Company and Genealogy.com. Reprints immigrant names from previously published books.

Indianola Immigrant Database <www.indianolabulletin.com/immigrant-database.htm> contains about 1,500 names of immigrants who, according to oral family lore or some written source, arrived at Indianola, Texas, before that port and all of its official arrival records were destroyed by a hurricane in 1886. The project is ongoing.

Irish Immigrants to North America, 1735–1871. CD-ROM #257 by Genealogical Publishing Company and Genealogy.com. Reprints Irish immigrant names from ten previously published books.

McManus, J. *Comal County, Texas, and New Braunfels, Texas, German Immigrant Ships, 1845-1846.* St. Louis: F. T. Ingmire, 1985. Over 2,000 passengers arriving on forty-one ships are enumerated and indexed.

Norlie, Olaf Morgan. *History of the Norwegian People in America.* Minneapolis: Augsburg Publishing House, 1925. Reprint by Haskell House Publishers, New York, 1973. Traces to the sixth generation the descendants of the 52/53 Norwegians (one born at sea) who came in 1825 on the ship *Restaurationen.* No index.

Olsson, Nils William. *Swedish Passenger Arrivals in New York, 1820–1850.* Chicago: Swedish Pioneer Historical Society, 1967. Covers all Swedes for port and period, with additional information for about one-third of them.

_____. *Swedish Passenger Arrivals in U.S. Ports, 1820-1850 (Except New York).* St. Paul: North Central Publishing Co., 1979. Complements the author's book on Swedish arrivals in New York.

Owen, Robert Edward, ed. *Luxembourgers in the New World.* 2 vols. Esch-sur-Alzette, Luxembourg: Editions-Reliures Schortgen, 1987. A reedition based on Nicholas Gonner's *Die Luxemburger in der Neuen Welt,* published in Dubuque, Iowa, 1889. More an ethnic history than published passenger arrival information, it contains the names of thousands of immigrants and states where they settled. Indexed.

Select Bibliography

Passenger and Immigration Lists: Baltimore, Sept. 2, 1820, to May 28, 1852. CD-ROM #259 by Genealogy.com. Alphabetical name index to National Archives Micropublication M255, *Passenger Lists of Vessels Arriving at Baltimore, 1820–1891*, rolls 1-8.

Passenger and Immigration Lists: Boston, 1821–1850. CD-ROM #256 by Genealogy.com. Alphabetical name index to National Archives Micropublication M277, *Passenger Lists of Vessels Arriving at Boston, 1820–1891*, rolls 1–36.

Passenger and Immigration Lists: New Orleans, 1820-1850. CD-ROM #358 by Genealogy.com. Alphabetical name index to National Archives Micropublication M259, *Passenger Lists of Vessels Arriving at New Orleans, 1820-1902*, rolls 1–33.

Passenger and Immigration Lists: New York, 1820-1850. CD-ROM #273 by Genealogy.com. Alphabetical name index to National Archives Micropublication M237, *Passenger Lists of Vessels Arriving at New York, 1820-1897*, rolls 1–95.

Passenger and Immigration Lists: Philadelphia, 1820–1850. CD-ROM #359 by Genealogy.com. Alphabetical name index to National Archives Micropublication M425, *Passenger Lists of Vessels Arriving at Philadelphia, 1800–1882*, rolls 30-71.

Prins, Edward. *Dutch and German Ships.* Holland, Mich.: published by the compiler, 1972. Passenger lists of many ships carrying Dutch and German immigrants to Atlantic ports, 1846–1855, especially those who settled the Holland colony in Michigan. No index.

Rasmussen, Louis J. *San Francisco Ship Passenger Lists.* 4 vols. Baltimore: Genealogical Publishing Co., 1978. Original San Francisco arrival lists prior to 1893 were destroyed by fire. Rasmussen "reconstructs" them by using other contemporary sources, 1850–1875.

Rieder, Milton P., and Norma Gaudet Rieder, eds. *New Orleans Ship Lists.* 2 vols. Metairie, La.: 1966 and 1968. Indexes New Orleans lists, 1 January 1820 through 23 June 1823, on microfilm at the National Archives.

Rockett, Charles Whitlock. *Some Shipboard Passengers of Captain John Rockett (1828–1841).* Mission Viejo, Calif.: the compiler, 1983. About 1,500 passengers aboard ships from Le Havre to New York. (A portion of at least one list—the list of the ship *Nile*, arrived 24 May 1830—was missed by the compiler.)

Rupp, Daniel L. *A Collection of Upwards of Thirty Thousand Names of German, Swiss, Dutch, French and Other Immigrants to Pennsylvania from 1727–1776.* Published originally in 1876. Reprint by Genealogical Publishing Co., Baltimore, 2000. This book complements *Pennsylvania German Pioneers* by Strassburger and Hinke, as it contains passengers of other nationalities.

Schlegel, Donald M. *Passengers from Ireland: Lists of Passengers Arriving at American Ports Between 1811 and 1817.* Baltimore: Genealogical Publishing Co., 1980.

Scottish Immigrants to North America, 1600s-1800s: Collected Works of David Dobson. CD-ROM #268 by Genealogical Publishing Company and Genealogy.com. Reprints ten titles by David Dobson, one of which is a seven-volume set.

Select Bibliography

Strassburger, Ralph Beaver, comp., and William John Hinke, ed. *Pennsylvania German Pioneers: A Publication of the Original Lists of Arrivals in the Port of Philadelphia from 1727 to 1808.* 3 vols. Norristown, Pa.: Pennsylvania German Society, 1934. First volume indexes lists of 1727–1784; second contains facsimiles of passenger signatures found in lists of 1727–1775; third indexes lists of 1785–1808.

Swierenga, Robert P., comp. *Dutch Immigrants in U.S. Ship Passenger Manifests, 1820-1880: An Alphabetical Listing by Household Heads and Independent Persons.* 2 vols. Wilmington, Del.: Scholarly Research, Inc., 1983. Dutch arrivals taken from lists in the National Archives. Fills gaps in National Archives indexes.

Taylor, Maureen A. *Rhode Island Passenger Lists.* Baltimore: Genealogical Publishing Co., 1995. Three alphabetical listings: (1) alien registration lists for Providence, 1798–1808; (2) customs passenger lists for Providence, 1820–1872; (3) customs passenger lists for Bristol and Warren, 1820–1871. Very valuable as much of this information—gathered at the Rhode Island Historical Society—is not found in National Archives records.

Tepper, Michael H., ed. *Emigrants to Pennsylvania, 1641–1819: A Consolidation of Ship Passenger Lists from the Pennsylvania Magazine of History and Biography.* Baltimore: Genealogical Publishing Co., 1975.

_____. *Immigrants to the Middle Colonies: A Consolidation of Ship Passenger Lists and Associated Data from the New York Genealogical and Biographical Record.* Baltimore: Genealogical Publishing Co., 1978.

_____. *New World Immigrants: A Consolidation of Ship Passenger Lists and Associated Data from Periodical Literature.* 2 vols. Baltimore: Genealogical Publishing Co., 1979. Includes the names of about 27,500 immigrants, mostly English, Irish, Scottish, German, Swiss, French, Dutch, Norwegian, and Germans from Russia, who came between 1618 and 1878.

_____. *Passenger Arrivals at the Port of Baltimore, 1820–1834: From Customs Passenger Lists.* Baltimore: Genealogical Publishing Co., 1982. Alphabetical listing made from the microfilmed lists in the National Archives.

_____. *Passenger Arrivals at the Port of Philadelphia, 1800–1819: The Philadelphia "Baggage Lists."* Baltimore: Genealogical Publishing Co., 1986. Alphabetical listing of about 40,000 passengers from the microfilmed lists at the National Archives.

_____. *Passengers to America: A Consolidation of Ship Passenger Lists from the New England Historical and Genealogical Register.* Baltimore: Genealogical Publishing Co., 1977.

Yoder, Don, ed. *Pennsylvania German Immigrants, 1709–1786: Lists Consolidated from Yearbooks of The Pennsylvania German Folklore Society.* Baltimore: Genealogical Publishing Co., 1980.

_____, ed. *Rhineland Emigrants: Lists of German Settlers in Colonial America.* Baltimore: Genealogical Publishing Co., 1981. About 4,000 names excerpted from articles in *Pennsylvania Folklife*, *1966–1977*.

Zimmerman, Gary J., and Marion Wolfert, comps. *German Immigrants: Lists of Passengers Bound from Bremen to New York.* 4 vols. Baltimore: Genealogical Publishing Co., 1985–93. Since lists of emigrants sailing from Bremen were destroyed, this work "reconstructs" lists of some German passengers on ships from Bremen to New York, 1847–1871, using arrival lists in the National Archives.

Published Departure Lists and Indexes

Blaha, Albert J. *Passenger Lists for Galveston, 1850–1855.* Houston: the author, 1985. Translation of lists printed in Hamburg and Bremen newspapers. Indexed. This material has been incorporated into the Galveston Immigrant Database at the Texas Seaport Museum <www.tsm-elissa.org>.

Bremen Passenger Lists, 1920–1939, are currently being transcribed and up-loaded to the Internet at http://db.genealogy.net/maus/gate/shiplists.cgi, with a search engine to help find one passenger among the many.

Burgert, Annette K. *Eighteenth Century Emigrants from German-Speaking Lands to North America.* Breinigsville, Pa.: Pennsylvania German Society, 1983 (vol. 16) and 1985 (vol. 19). Information on German-speaking emigrants from the Northern Kraichgau and Western Palatinate.

Coldham, Peter Wilson. *Bonded Passengers to America.* 9 vols. Baltimore: Genealogical Publishing Co., 1983–85. A monumental resource. Names of thousands of English and Irish sent to the colonies as bonded passengers. (Many other volumes listing emigrants to America compiled by Coldham are available as books and CD-ROMs.)

Dobson, David. *Directory of Scottish Settlers in North America, 1625–1825.* 6 vols. Baltimore: Genealogical Publishing Co., 1984. Based on published sources and documents in British archives, names thousands of Scottish emigrants.

Hall, Charles M. *Antwerp Emigration Index*. Salt Lake City: Heritage International, 1986. Lists 5,100 emigrants from Germany, Switzerland, Italy, Belgium, France and the Netherlands who embarked from Antwerp during 1855.

Hamburg Emigration Lists, 1850-1934, are now being transcribed and uploaded to the Internet <www.hamburg.de/LinkToYourRoots/english/welcome.htm>, beginning with 1890, with a search engine.

Kaminkow, Jack, and Marian Kaminkow. *A List of Emigrants from England to America*. Baltimore: Magna Carta Book Co., 1981. Three thousand names transcribed from microfilms of the original records at the Guildhall, London.

Mitchell, Brian, comp. *Irish Passenger Lists, 1803–1806*. Baltimore: Genealogical Publishing Co., 1995. Copied from the Hardwicke Papers in the British Library, London, about 4,500 passengers who left on 109 sailings out of Dublin, Belfast, Londonderry, and Newry.

_____. *Irish Passenger Lists, 1847–1871*. Baltimore: Genealogical Publishing Co., 1988. Lists created by two shipping lines, J.&J. Cook and McCorkell, recording crossings from Londonderry to America.

Schenk, Trudy, Ruth Froelke, and Inge Bork, comps. *The Wuerttemberg Emigration Index*. 7 vols. Salt Lake City: Ancestry, Inc., 1986–93. About 84,000 persons who applied to emigrate from Wuerttemberg, 1750–1900, with intended destination of each. All seven volumes are available on one CD-ROM.

Schrader-Muggenthaler, Cornelia. *Alsace Emigration Book*. 2 vols. Apollo, Pa.: Closson Press, 1989–91. Lists about 21,500 emigrants who left Alsace in the late eighteenth through late nineteenth centuries.

Select Bibliography

_____. *Baden Emigration Book*. Apollo, Pa.: Closson Press, 1992. Lists about 7,000 eighteenth- and nineteenth-century emigrants who came to America from Baden and Alsace.

Smith, Clifford Neal. *Reconstructed Passenger Lists for 1850: Hamburg to Australia, Brazil, Canada, Chile, and the United States.* 4 vols. McNeal, Ariz.: Westland Publications, 1980. "Reconstructed" lists based on Hamburg Emigration Lists.

Wareing, John. *Emigrants to America: Indentured Servants Recruited in London, 1718–1733.* Baltimore: Genealogical Publishing Co., 1985. About 1,500 names.

Lists of Ships Arriving at American Ports

Bangerter, Lawrence B. *The Compass: A Concise and Factual Compilation of All Vessels and Sources Listed, with Reference Made of All of Their Voyages and Some Dates of Registration.* 2 vols. Logan, Utah: Everton Publishers, 1983–90. Vol. 1 contains ships arriving at Baltimore, 1820–1891; vol. 2 contains ships arriving at Boston, 1820-1860.

Dobson, David. *Ships from Ireland to Early America, 1623–1850.* Baltimore: Genealogical Publishing Co., 1999. Alphabetical listing of many ships compiled from published and original sources.

_____. *Ships from Scotland to America, 1628–1828.* Baltimore: Genealogical Publishing Co., 1998. Alphabetical listing of many ships compiled from published and original sources.

Filby, P. William. *Passenger and Immigration Lists Bibliography, 1538–1900: Being a Guide to Published Lists of Arrivals in the United States and Canada,* 2nd ed. Detroit: Gale Research Co., 1988. Most comprehensive list available of ships whose lists have appeared in published literature.

Morton Allan Directory of European Passenger Steamship Arrivals at the Port of New York, 1890–1930, and at the Ports of Baltimore, Boston, and Philadelphia, 1904–1926. New York: Immigration Information Bureau, 1931. Reprint by Genealogical Publishing Co., Baltimore, 1979. Dates of arrival for every vessel, by steamship line. This book has been up-loaded to the Internet by Anthony J. Cimorelli at <www.cimorelli.com/safe/shipmenu.htm>, along with selected portions of National Archives Micropublication M1066, *Registers of Vessels Arriving at the Port of New York from Foreign Ports, 1789-1919.*

Registers of Vessels Arriving at the Port of New York from Foreign Ports, 1789–1919. National Archives Micropublication M1066. Provides original port of embarkation and date of arrival for all passenger vessels; does not indicate intermediate ports of call.

Steuart, Bradley W. *Passenger Ships Arriving in New York Harbor (1820–1850).* Bountiful, Utah: Precision Indexing, 1991. Drawn from National Archives Micropublication M1066, *Registers of Vessels Arriving at the Port of New York from Foreign Ports, 1789-1919.*

Alternative Sources for Colonial Arrival Information

Anderson, Robert Charles. *The Great Migration Begins, 1620–1633.* 3 vols. Boston: New England Historic Genealogical Society, 1998. Monumental work documenting immigrants to New England and the first three generations of their progeny.

Coldham, Peter Wilson. *Settlers of Maryland, 1679–1700. Settlers of Maryland, 1701–1730. Settlers of Maryland, 1731–1750.* 3 vols. Baltimore: Genealogical Publishing Co., 1995–96. Abstracted from colonial Maryland land grants.

Select Bibliography

Gibb, Carson. *A Supplement to The Early Settlers of Maryland: 8,680 Entries Correcting Omissions and Errors in Gust Skordas's The Early Settlers of Maryland*. Annapolis, Md.: Maryland State Archives, 1997.

Holcomb, Brent H. *Petitions for Land from the South Carolina Council Journals, 7 vols.* Columbia, S.C.: SCMAR, 1996-1999. Many of these petitions, which cover 1734-1774, are from immigrants, mostly German and Irish, and make reference to their year of arrival and ship.

Hotten, John Camden. *The Original Lists of Persons of Quality . . . 1600-1700*. London: The Public Record Office, 1874. Reprint by Genealogical Publishing Co., Baltimore, 1974. This classic work about early Virginia settlers has been updated and expanded in Peter Wilson Coldham's many books.

Hume, Robert. *Early Child Immigrants to Virginia, 1618–1642*. Baltimore: Magna Carta Book Co., 1986. Transcribed from the records of Bridewell Royal Hospital, names 468 street children sent to the colonies at the request of the Virginia Company, mostly in the 1620s.

Johnson, Amandus. *The Swedish Settlements on the Delaware, 1638–1664*. 2 vols. 1911. Reprint by the Genealogical Publishing Co., Baltimore, 1969.

Knittle, Walter Allen. *Early Eighteenth Century Palatine Emigration*. Published originally in 1937. Reprint by the Genealogical Publishing Co., Baltimore, 1965. About 12,000 Palatines, mostly to Pennsylvania, North Carolina, and New York.

Nugent, Nell Marion, comp. *Cavaliers and Pioneers: Abstracts of Virginia Land Patents and Grants. 3 vols., 1623–1732.* Richmond: Virginia State Library. Now expanded to 6 vols., 1623–1820. Richmond: Virginia Genealogical Society.

Skordas, Gust. *The Early Settlers of Maryland: An Index to Names of Immigrants Compiled from Records of Land Patents, 1633–1680, in the Hall of Records, Annapolis, Maryland.* Baltimore: Genealogical Publishing Co., 1968. This work has been corrected in Carson Gibb's *A Supplement to The Early Settlers of Maryland,* cited previously.

Images and Information About Sailing Vessels and Steamships

Anuta, Michael J. *Ships of Our Ancestors.* Menominee, Mich.: Ships of Our Ancestors, 1983. Photos of 880 ships that brought immigrants to the United States, 1819–1960. Bibliography on ships and ship-building.

Bonsor, N.R.P. *North Atlantic Seaway.* 4 vols. London: T. Stephenson and Sons, 1955. Supplement, 1960. Enl. and rev. ed. by Douglas, David and Charles, Vancouver, Canada, 1975. Illustrated history of the passenger services linking the Old World with the New.

Culver, Henry B., and Gordon Grant. *The Book of Old Ships.* Garden City, N.Y.: Garden City Publishing Co., Inc., 1924. Descriptions and drawings of the different kinds of sailing vessels.

Kinshipsprints <www.kinshipsprints.com> offers reproductions of prints of over 300 steamships.

Kludas, Arnold. *Great Passenger Ships of the World.* 6 vols. Translated from original German edition of 1972–74 by Charles Hodges.

Cambridge, England: Patrick Stephens, 1975–1977. Information and photos of all major passenger ships, 1858–1977.

Mariner's Museum, Newport News, Va. <www.mariner.org> has many pictures of old sailing vessels and steamships.

Maxtone-Graham, John. *The Only Way to Cross*. New York: Macmillan Co., 1972. Steamships: their construction, grandeur, and mystique.

Mystic Seaport, Mystic, Conn. <www.mysticseaport.org> a museum that holds many pictures of old sailing vessels and steamships.

Peabody Essex Museum, Salem, Mass. <www.pem.org> has many pictures of old sailing vessels and steamships.

Smith, Eugene W. *Passenger Ships of the World*. Boston: George H. Dean Co., 1978. Thumbnail sketches of ships, arranged by geographic area where they operated.

Steamship Historical Society of America, Baltimore, Md. <www.ubalt.edu/archives/ship/ship.htm> holds images of 200,000 steamships, as well as other steamship materials and memorabilia.

Texas Seaport Museum, Galveston <www.tsm-elissa.org> has a "Galveston Immigrant Database" containing 130,000 names of people who arrived at the port of Galveston, 1846-1948.

TheShipsList <www.theshipslist.com> Established to assist those seeking information on the vessels which brought their ancestors to a new home, be that the United States, Canada, Australia, or another part of the world.

The Immigrant Experience

Brasseaux, Carl A. *The Founding of New Acadia: The Beginnings of Acadian Life in Louisiana, 1765–1803*. Baton Rouge: Louisiana State University Press, 1987. Just one example of the huge corpus of "ethnic histories" to be found in libraries. These provide much detail regarding the establishment of different ethnic groups in America, providing the historical background against which each immigrant ancestor may be examined to understand his or her unique story.

Carmack, Sharon DeBartolo. *Discovering Your Immigrant and Ethnic Ancestors*. Cincinnati: Betterway Books, 2000. Excellent historical overview of the major ethnic groups in America, with notes on how to conduct research on each; extensive bibliographies.

_____. *The Ebetino and Vallarelli Family History*. Anundsen Publishing Co., 1990. Good example of a well-researched and well-written story of a turn-of-the-century immigrant family.

Colletta, John Philip. "Discovering the Real Stories of Your Immigrant Ancestors." Audiotape of lecture, W7: Repeat Performance <www.audiotapes.com>, 2000. Three examples demonstrate how to combine information from oral family lore, public and private records, and material culture to appreciate each immigrant ancestor as a distinct individual with a unique story.

_____. *Only a Few Bones: A True Account of the Rolling Fork Tragedy and Its Aftermath*. Washington, D.C.: Direct Descent, 2000. Another meticulously researched story of immigrant ancestors. Traces a family of German-speakers from Lorraine, France, to Buffalo, New York (1830), and then down to Mississippi after the Civil War, where the author's great-great-grandfather died under mysterious circumstances (1873) investigated by authorities as mass murder, robbery, arson, and insurance fraud.

Daniels, Roger. *Coming to America: A History of Immigration and Ethnicity in American Life.* New York: HarperCollins, 1990. Excellent overview.

Fischer, David Hacket. *Albion's Seed: Four British Folkways in America.* New York: Oxford University Press, 1989. Extraordinary demonstration of how varied English emigration to America was between 1629 and 1775, encompassing Puritans to Massachusetts Bay, cavaliers and indentured servants to Virginia, Quakers to the Delaware Valley, and emigrants from North Britain to America's backcountry.

Guillet, Edwin C. *The Great Migration: The Atlantic Crossing by Sailing Ship Since 1770,* rev. ed. Toronto: University of Toronto Press, 1963. Vivid and detailed account of what the voyage was like. Rich bibliography.

Handlin, Oscar. *The Uprooted: The Epic Story of the Great Migrations that Made the American People.* New York: Grosset & Dunlap, 1951. Describes the immigrants' encounter with American society: how it affected them and how they adjusted.

_____, ed. *Immigration as a Factor in American History.* Englewood Cliffs, N.J.: Prentice-Hall, Inc., 1959. A selection of readings by different authors. Explores what immigration has meant to America over the years.

Hansen, Marcus Lee. *The Atlantic Migration, 1607-1860,* rev. ed. Cambridge, Mass.: Harvard University Press, 1951. Describes emigrants leaving their European homelands. Pages 172–198 discuss which ports of embarkation in Europe, and which ports of arrival in the United States, were used by various national groups in the nineteenth century.

Hinchliff, Helen. "Michael Mumper of Pennsylvania: Reconstructing the Origins and Circumstances of an Immigrant Ancestor." *National Genealogical Society Quarterly* 77, no. 1 (March 1989): 5–21. How to research and write an eighteenth-century immigrant ancestor's story.

Hopkins, Albert A. *The Scientific American Handbook of Travel.* New York: Munn & Co., 1910. Photographs and information about crossing the Atlantic in the early twentieth century: fares, menus, what to pack, etc.

Jones, Hank Z, Jr. *More Palatine Families: Some Immigrants to the Middle Colonies, 1717–1776, and Their European Origins.* San Diego: the author, 1991. Exemplary research in linking American colonists to their European origins. Author has done other similar books.

Kraut, Alan M. *The Huddled Masses: The Immigrant in American Society, 1880–1921.* Arlington Heights, Ill.: Harlan Davidson, Inc., 1982. How immigrant groups adjusted to American society. Challenges stereotypical images of immigrants.

Maire, Camille. *L'Emigration des Lorrains en Amérique, 1815–1870.* Metz, France: Presse de l'Université de Metz, 1980. Just one example of the kind of scholarly studies available now about the emigration patterns of specific national and ethnic and religious groups.

Miller, Olga K. *Migration, Emigration, Immigration; Principally to the United States.* 2 vols. Logan, Utah: Everton Publishers, 1974. Patterns of migration, ports used by different groups, etc.

Steele, Oliver G. *The Traveler's Directory and Emigrant's Guide; Containing General Descriptions of Different Routes Through the States of New York, Ohio, Indiana, Illinois, and the Territory of Michigan, 1832.* Revised editions published in 1836, 1844, and 1849. Known simply as "Steele's Western Guide," this work describes routes and modes of transportation used by immigrants in the mid-nineteenth century. It has been microfilmed.

Tracing Immigrant Origins. Salt Lake City: Family History Library, 1992. This 31-page "Research Outline" is valuable for not over-looking any resource that might help determine an immigrant ancestor's native town. Online at the Family History Library's website <www.familysearch.org>.

Ellis Island

Bolino, August C. *The Ellis Island Source Book.* Washington, D.C.: Historical Press, 1985. The definitive bibliography of published and unpublished resources pertaining to Ellis Island and its history.

Novotny, Ann. *Strangers at the Door.* Riverside, Conn.: The Chatham Press, 1971. Describes the immigration process at the port of New York: Castle Garden, 1855–90; Barge Office, 1890–91; and Ellis Island, 1892–1924. Bibliography of major works on immigration.

Pitkin, Thomas M. *Keepers of the Gate: A History of Ellis Island.* New York: New York University Press, 1975. A thorough and authoritative history of Ellis Island.

Roberts, Jayare. "Ellis Island and the Making of America." *Genealogical Journal, an international publication of the Utah Genealogical Association*, vol. 23, nos. 2 and 3 (1995).

Szucs, Loretto Dennis. *Ellis Island, Gateway to America*, rev. ed. Salt Lake City: Ancestry, Inc., 2000. Informative overview of Ellis Island, the immigrant experience, and pertinent records for genealogists to research their own immigrant ancestors.

Tifft, Wilton S. *Ellis Island*. New York: W.W. Norton & Co., 1971. Collection of historic photographs of the island and its immigrants, plus modern photographs by Wilton Tifft of the buildings before their restoration as a museum. Text by Thomas Dunne.

_____. *Ellis Island*. Chicago: Contemporary Books, 1990. Full history of the island, richly illustrated.

Index

A

American Family Immigration History
Center website
    alternative search engines for, 84
    finding your ancestor, 83, 83–84
    summary of contents, 18, 82
ancestry.com, 16
archives.ca, 116

B

Barge Office processing center, 124, 125
births at sea, 45
Black American genealogy, 30–32
Bohemian ancestors, sources of infor-
    mation on, 15
Bremen passenger lists, 99–101

C

Canada, immigration via, 114–16, 115
Castle Garden receiving station,
    123–24, 125
CD-ROM indexes
    applying principles of sound
        methodology to, 79
    convenience of, 79
    examples of, 80–81
    limitations of, 81–82
census records, as sources of passenger
    information, 13–14
Chinese Exclusion Act (1882), 38, 111
Chinese passenger lists, 111–12
Church of Jesus Christ of Latter-day
    Saints website, 16, 88–89
cimorelli.com, 88
city directories, as sources of passenger

information, 16
civil records, as sources of passenger
    information, 13
crew lists, 110–11
Customs Passenger Lists/Manifests. *See*
    passenger arrival records, 1820 and
    later
Cyndi's List of Genealogy Sites on the
    Internet website, 16, 33, 85

D

daddezio.com, 86
db.genealogy.net, 100
deaths at sea, 45
Delaware River Valley ancestors,
    records of colonial immigrant
    arrivals, 22
departure ports
    determining your ancestor's
        probable port of departure,
        98–99
    southern and eastern European
        ancestors, 3
departure records, U.S. port, 117–18
documents, personal and family, as
    sources of passenger information,
    12–13

E

eastern European ancestors, post-1921
    departure ports, 3
Ellis Island
    closing of, 126–27
    destruction by fire and loss of
        records, 125

Index

Index

About the Author

John Philip Colletta is one of America's most popular genealogical lecturers. Based in Washington, D.C., he teaches at the National Archives, Smithsonian Institution, and area universities. He is also a faculty member of the Institute of Genealogy and Historical Research (Birmingham, Ala.) and Salt Lake Institute of Genealogy (Salt Lake City), and has been a course coordinator and instructor for other genealogical institutes as well. His publications include numerous articles, two manuals, and *Only a Few Bones*, a meticulously documented narrative that traces the Ring family from Lorraine, France, to Buffalo, New York, and then Mississippi, where the author's great-great-grandfather died under mysterious circumstances investigated by authorities as mass murder, robbery, arson, and insurance fraud. Dr. Colletta has appeared on local and national radio and television, and is featured in *Ancestors*, the PBS series. He earned his Ph.D. in Medieval French from The Catholic University of America. His lectures and banquet speeches are famous for their clarity, humor, wit, and warmth.

Finding Your Immigrant Ancestor's Ship

1

- **Full original name**
- **Approximate age at arrival**
- **Approximate date of arrival**

Where can you find this information?

- Oral family tradition
- Personal and family documents: passports, letters, diaries, Bible inscriptions, funeral cards, etc.
- Civil and religious records: military service, censuses, naturalization, marriage, tombstones, etc.
- Published works in libraries: genealogies, local and ethnic histories, professional directories, etc.
- Websites and e-mail

Arrival Prior to 1820

Many lists of passengers bound for, or arriving in, America prior to 1820, as well as other types of colonial and early federal records containing immigrant information, have appeared in published form. Search the name indexes to this published historical material found in libraries.

2

Arrival Between 1820 and the 1950s

Lists of passengers arriving in the United States from 1820 through the 1950s are available on microfilm at the National Archives, Family History Library in Salt Lake City, and larger public libraries nationwide. Search the National Archives name indexes to those lists or, if necessary, use one of the alternative finding aids.

Name Indexes to Published Arrival Information

If all you know are the three basic facts, search for your ancestor's name in any index to published arrival information. Also search Cyndi's List at <www.cyndislist.com> for links to pertinent Websites.

Or

If you also know your ancestor's nationality, search for your ancestor in indexes compiled by nationality.

3

Finding Aids

- **National Archives Name Indexes** are compiled by port for U.S. ports on the Atlantic, Pacific, Great Lakes, and Gulf Coast, but they do not cover every year for every port. Search port-by-port for your ancestor's name until process of elimination has yielded a few likely candidates.

Or

If you also know your ancestor's "group" or place of settlement, search for your ancestor in indexes compiled by religious or otherwise identifiable group, or by geographic place of settlement.

Or

If you also know your ancestor's port of arrival, search for your ancestor in indexes compiled by port of arrival.

Or

If you also know the name of your ancestor's ship, search for that ship's name in a bibliography of published passenger arrival records. If the name appears and the arrival date coincides with your ancestor's, scan the list for your ancestor's name.

Or

If your ancestor was a slave, he or she was not listed by name in the cargo manifest. However, circumstantial evidence of your ancestor's ship may be obtained if you can learn where, when, and by whom the slave was first purchased. You can then search records pertaining to that place and time and slaveholder.

- **Published Book Indexes** focus on a particular port or nationality or time period, but they fill in the gaps in the National Archives indexes. Search them just as you would search the name indexes to pre-1820 published arrival information.

- **CD-ROM Indexes** also help fill in the gaps in National Archives indexes and published book indexes. Search for your ancestor's name in any CD that covers your ancestor's approximate date of arrival.

- **Websites.** Visit <www.cyndislist.com> for links to many Web sites containing passenger arrival lists and related resources. If your ancestor arrived at New York between 1892 and 1924, visit <www.ellisislandrecords.org>.

- **Lists of Ships Arriving at U.S. Ports.** If none of the above resources help and you know the name of your ancestor's ship, its precise date of arrival, or its overseas port of departure, consult lists of ships arriving at U.S. ports (such as Registers of Vessels Arriving at the Port of New York, 1789–1919, on microfilm, and the book Morton Allan Directory of European Passenger Steamship Arrivals), note which ships arrived when your ancestor did, and then search the lists of those ships for your ancestor's name.

- **Emigration Records.** If none of the above resources help, and you know your ancestor's most probable overseas port of departure, look for the emigration records of that port. If you find an emigration record for your ancestor, it will state his or her ship's name, date of departure, and port of destination. You then search the arrival records for that port for that ship, and scan the list for your ancestor's name.

The Passenger List

When you find your ancestor's name in the index, access the cited published arrival information or microfilmed passenger arrival list. Then read the record carefully to find the name of your ancestor. Double-check what you find against your ancestor's full, original name, approximate age at arrival, and approximate date of arrival to be certain you have found your ancestor.

4